FIVE MINUTE BIOGRAPHIES

FIVE MINUTE BIOGRAPHIES

By DALE CARNEGIE

Author of
How to Win Friends and Influence People,
Little Known Facts About Well Known People,
The Unknown Lincoln

ILLUSTRATED

SOUTHERN PUBLISHERS, Inc.

NEW YORK, N. Y. ∽ KINGSPORT, TENN.

PRINTED IN THE UNITED STATES OF AMERICA

CONTENTS

CONTENTS

CONTENTS

8 CONTENTS

This book is dedicated to a success-
ful man who is never in a hurry

WARREN S. BARLOW

MARTIN JOHNSON
Lions chewed up his front tires

THREE LITTLE WORDS—"CAN YOU COOK?"
LED HIM TO THE ENDS OF THE EARTH

MARTIN JOHNSON, who photographed thousands of lions in the wilds of Africa, killed only two. He told me that during twenty months of his last stay in Africa, he saw more lions than he had ever seen before; yet he never fired a gun once. In fact, he didn't even carry a gun.

Some African explorers like to come back and tell about their blood-curdling experiences; but Martin Johnson believed that he or any other man who really knows the wild animals of Africa can walk from Cairo to the Cape armed with nothing more deadly than a bamboo walking stick and never suffer any harm.

He also told me that the last time he went to Africa, he took along a fine radio set so he could listen to programs from America. He said he listened a great deal for the first month or two, and then he got so tired of listening to long, blatant commercial announcements, that he didn't turn on the radio for months at a time.

Martin Johnson started roaming the world when he was fourteen years old. His father was a jeweler in Independence, Kansas, and when Martin was a boy, he used to unpack the crates that came from the far-flung corners of the compass. He was fascinated by the strange, colorful names on the labels—Paris, Geneva, Barcelona,

Budapest—and he determined to put the dust of those towns under his heel. So one day he ran away, tramped over the United States, and finally shipped on a cattle boat to Europe. Landing in the old world, he worked at anything he could find; but he couldn't always find work. He went hungry in Brussels; in Brest, he stood gazing out across the Atlantic, discouraged and homesick; and in London, he had to sleep in packing boxes. In order to get back to America and Kansas, he hid himself as a stowaway in the lifeboat of a steamship bound for New York.

Then something happened which changed the course of his whole existence, and set him out on trails of glamorous adventure. An engineer on the boat showed him a magazine containing an article by Jack London. Jack London told in this article how he intended to make a trip around the world in a little thirty-foot boat called the *Snark*.

As soon as Johnson arrived home in Independence, he wrote a letter to Jack London. He poured out his soul in eight feverish pages, and begged to go along on that trip. "I've already been abroad," he wrote. "I started from Chicago with $5.50 in my pocket, and when I got back, I still had twenty-five cents."

Two weeks passed—two weeks of nerve-wracking suspense. And then came a telegram from Jack London. It contained only three words—three words that changed Martin Johnson's life. "Can you cook?" the telegram inquired with telegraphic abruptness and brevity.

Could he cook? Why, he couldn't even cook rice. But he wired back precisely three words—"Just try me"— then he went out and got himself a job in the kitchen of a restaurant.

And when the *Snark* finally sailed across the rippling

waters in San Francisco bay, and nosed her way out into the Pacific, Martin Johnson was aboard as chief cook and bottle washer, and his newly acquired culinary knowledge enabled him to make bread, omelets, gravy, soup, and even pudding. It was also his job to buy the provisions for the trip, and he calculated that he took along enough salt and pepper and other spices to last a normal crew something like two hundred years.

He learned to navigate during that trip. He thought he was an expert navigator. So one day, just to show how smart he was, he tried to locate the position of the ship on the map. By that time, the *Snark* was in mid-Pacific swept along by billowing sails in the direction of Honolulu; but according to his nautical calculations, the ship was located squarely in the middle of the Atlantic Ocean!

But he didn't give a whoop if his calculations were all cock-eyed. He was living the gay, adventurous life every boy dreams of living. Nothing could daunt his enthusiasm. Once the crew ran out of water for two weeks and nearly perished under a sizzling sun—a sun so blasted hot that the pitch in the deck seams bubbled and boiled like soft molasses!

Almost thirty happy years have passed since then—years packed with action, for Martin Johnson sailed the seven seas and roamed all over the world from the coral islands of the South Seas to the jungles of darkest Africa. He made the first pictures of cannibals ever shown in this country. He photographed pigmies and giants, elephants and giraffes, and made pictures of all the wild life on the African veldt. He brought back a whole Noah's Ark full of fantastic creatures—brought 'em back on spools of celluloid film that have been unreeled upon thousands of moving picture screens. He captured an imperishable record of a perishing wild animal life—a photographic record that your great grandchildren may enjoy generations from now when many of the wild animals of Africa no longer exist.

Martin Johnson told me that a well-fed lion that has never been molested by man will pay no attention whatever to the scent of a human being. He had driven his automobile into the midst of a bunch of fifteen lions, and the lions just lay there and blinked like pussy cats. One lion even came over and started to chew the front tire. Another time, he drove his car so close to a lioness that she could have reached out and touched it with her paw—but she didn't so much as twitch a whisker.

I asked him: "Are you trying to tell me that a lion is really a *good-natured* beast?"

And he said: "Good heavens, no! The best way I know to commit suicide is to trust a lion. Why, you never know when he's going to become suspicious and turn on you. And there's nothing in the world more dangerous than a charging lion. It's just like having a hundred pounds of dynamite coming at you. A lion can travel forty feet at a single leap, and he can cover ground faster than Cavalcade on the home stretch."

I asked him what he considered his narrowest escape, and he said: "Oh, there have been lots of close calls. But they're all fun."

One of his closest calls was in the South Sea Islands, when he nearly ended up in a kettle of soup. That was when he was getting the first pictures of cannibals ever made.

White traders had been raiding the cannibal islands, kidnaping the natives and selling them into slavery. The cannibals were hostile and suspicious—and hungry. They had already killed a number of white men and seized their goods; and after sizing up Martin Johnson, they figured that this chap from Kansas would make a nice tender pot roast for Sunday dinner. So while he was busy talking to the chief and laying out the presents he had brought along, dozens of cannibals began to gather out of the forest and surround him. Help was miles away. He had a revolver, but he was outnumbered a hundred to one. A cold sweat of fear stood out on his forehead. His heart raced and pounded; but there was nothing to do but to try to appear calm and keep on talking. And all the time he was being crowded in by a ring of greedy cannibals licking their chops in anticipation. For the first time since he'd left Independence, Kansas, Martin Johnson began to think it might not have been a bad idea after all if he'd gone into the jewelry business with his father.

And then, just as the cannibals were about to rush, a miracle happened. Into the bay far below steamed a British patrol boat. The cannibals stared. They knew what that meant. Johnson stared too, hardly able to believe his own eyes. And then, with a low bow to the chief, he said: "You see, my ship has come after me. Glad to have met you all. Goodbye." And before anyone summoned enough courage to stop him, he made a dash for the shore.

FLORENZ ZIEGFELD

He borrowed $5,000.—to hire a private train!

HE KNEW THE TELEPHONE NUMBERS OF
MORE BEAUTIFUL GIRLS THAN ANY
MAN IN HISTORY

FOR twenty-four years, the *Ziegfeld Follies* blazed supreme over the firmament of Broadway. No other revue in the entire world was ever staged so lavishly or acclaimed with such roars of delight. No other revue ever made so much money, and no other revue ever lost so much money.

Florenz Ziegfeld knew the telephone numbers of more beautiful girls than any other man living. In his Blue Book of Beauty were listed the names, addresses, and telephone numbers of thousands of glamorous girls. Fifty or sixty aspiring young Venuses paraded before his critical glance every day.

He was proud of the fact that he was called the Glorifier of the American Girl. It was a title richly deserved. He often took some drab little girl no one had ever looked at twice and transformed her on the stage into a dazzling creature of mystery and seduction. Form and grace—these alone—were the coveted passport to the Ziegfeld stage. The glamor was supplied by Ziegfeld himself.

Ziegfeld was as regal in his extravagance as an Oriental potentate. He squandered millions of dollars on costumes, combing the markets of Europe and India and Asia for

the most beautiful fabrics money could buy. Even the
linings of dresses had to be of the finest silk, for he
claimed no woman could feel really beautiful unless she
had beautiful cloth against her skin.

In order to get just the proper hats for a certain cowboy number he had in mind, he postponed the production of *Show Boat* for three entire months. Once, after
he had spent a quarter of a million dollars on a production, he closed it after one performance, because he felt
it was unworthy of the glorious Ziegfeld tradition.

He did everything on a lavish scale. Although he com-
municated with hundreds of people daily, he never troubled to dictate a letter. Telegrams and cables fluttered in
his wake like autumn leaves in a gale of wind. Wherever
he went, he carried with him a telegraph blank. He used
to get on the train at Grand Central Station and use up a
whole pad of telegraph blanks before he reached 125th
Street.

Incredible as it seems, he actually sat in the orchestra
pit during rehearsals and sent telegrams to the actors
across the footlights. He sent telegrams to people who
were within range of his voice. He once leaned out of
his window and yelled at the man in the window opposite: "Say, I sent you a telegram. Why haven't you
answered it?"

It was almost impossible for him to walk past a telephone booth without stopping to call up a dozen people;
and he got out of bed almost every morning at six o'clock
in order to telephone to his staff.

He could scheme for hours to save seventeen or eighteen dollars; and the next day, he'd drop a hundred thousand dollars in Wall Street without batting an eye. He
once borrowed five thousand dollars from Ed Wynn,
and spent that five thousand dollars of borrowed money

to hire a private train to carry him across the continent.

He made women feel beautiful by the sheer power of his chivalry and consideration. On opening night, every girl in his chorus received a box of flowers from him. Even old and half-demented women who applied to him for jobs were treated with the same consideration he showed to all the rest.

He paid his most famous stars an average of $5,000. a week; often, at the end of the season they had more money in the bank than he himself had.

When he started in the show business, chorus girls were getting $30. a week; but under his profligate reign, feminine pulchritude reached a market price of $125. a week.

Ziegfeld's first venture into show business was made at the precocious age of fourteen. Running away from home, he became a trick rider and fancy shooter in Buffalo Bill's Wild West Show.

At the age of twenty-five, he was cleaning up a fortune as manager to Sandow, the husky strong man of the naughty Nineties.

Two years later, he was in London—broke—without a shilling to his name. He'd staked his luck at Monte Carlo, and with a turn of the wheel, he had lost his shirt.

Being penniless never worried this great entrepreneur. By the sheer witchery of his manner, he got together another show and sailed back in triumph to America with the most sensational star in Europe—the vivacious, scintillating, and palpitating Anna Held—the Mae West of her day.

The most canny producers in America had been cabling and pleading with Anna Held to come to New York. They had tempted her with extravagant offers. Yet it was Florenz Ziegfeld, only twenty-seven years old, practically unknown, and without a dime in his pocket, who walked into her dressing room, charmed her, got her name on a contract, and started skyrocketing to fame.

Anna Held was an immediate sensation. She took America by storm. Corsets, face powder, hats, perfumes, horses, cocktails, puppies, and cigars were named in her honor. She was toasted in champagne from coast to coast. And within a year, Florenz Ziegfeld married her.

Many years later, after he had divorced Anna Held, he fell ecstatically in love with Billie Burke. The very day after he met her, he bought out an entire flower shop and sent the complete stock to her home—sent her everything from sweet peas and orchids and carnations to the orange trees in the window. And when Billie Burke told him that she had tried to thank him by telephone, but had not been able to because his line was busy, he had a golden phone installed, with a special ring, for her private use.

Ziegfeld loved indecision. He hated to make up his mind. He used to keep a box of licorice drops on his desk; and when a friend asked him if he really liked licorice, he said: "I'll tell you why I eat them. They're all black, so I don't have to make up my mind which color I like best."

He hired the most famous comedians in the world for his Follies; but he himself never laughed at their antics. Neither Ed Wynn nor Eddie Cantor nor Will Rogers could make him crack a smile. He was so cool that his actors gave him the nickname of "Ice Water."

For twenty-four years, the opening night of the Follies was something of an event in roaring old New York. Limousines jammed the street; silk hats and ermine wraps thronged the lobby; and sharp-witted speculators made tired business men pay as high as $300. for a pair of seats in the front row. Backstage was filled with clamor and tumult. Wardrobe mistresses and messenger boys bumped into each other; comedians with stage fright muttered in the wings; and chorus girls hunted frantically for clothes. In the mad whirl, there was only one man who remained calm, cool and composed—that man was Ziegfeld. New York's sophisticated first nighters put on their tails and white ties for the auspicious occasion; but Ziegfeld himself appeared in a plain gray business suit. He didn't even allow himself the luxury of a seat. He watched the show from the stairs that led to the balcony.

When Wall Street crashed in 1929, it was lights and final curtain for the career of Ziegfeld the great Glorifier. From that time on, the magician who had lavished millions on tinsel and glitter for the gayest pageant in the world, could hardly raise the money to pay his rent. The last Follies was staged with funds partly supplied by his own stars and employees.

Ziegfeld died in 1932 in California, and as he slipped into the delirium of death, he imagined he was directing a revue. His stage was a white hospital room, his orchestra was only a radio; and for a stage crew, he had nothing but his terrified valet. His lips were parched, and his eyes were glowing with fever, but he sat up in bed and shouted his directions to an invisible cast.

"Curtain!" he cried. "Fast music! Lights! Ready for the last finale!" And finally he murmured: "Great! The show looks good. . . . The show . . . looks . . . good."

HOWARD THURSTON

He slept on a grating in back of a theatre and dreamed
of baffling the world

THE MISSIONARY WHO GOT ON THE WRONG TRAIN—AND BECAME A FAMOUS MAGICIAN

ONE cold night, half a century ago, a crowd was pouring out of McVicker's Theatre in Chicago. It was a laughing, happy crowd—a crowd that had been entertained by Alexander Herrmann, the great magician of that day.

A shivering newsboy stood on the sidewalk, trying to sell copies of the *Chicago Tribune* to the crowd. But he was having a tough time of it. He had no overcoat, he had no home, and he had no money to pay for a bed. That night, after the crowd faded away, he wrapped himself in newspapers and slept on top of an iron grating which was warmed slightly by the furnace in the basement, in an alley back of the theatre.

As he lay there, hungry and shivering, he vowed that he too would be a magician. He longed to have crowds applauding him, wear a fur-lined coat, and have girls waiting for him at the stage door. So he made a solemn vow that when he was a famous magician, he would come back and play as a headliner in the same theatre.

That boy was Howard Thurston—and twenty years later he did precisely that. After his performance he went out in the alley and found his initials where he had carved them on the back of the theatre a quarter of a century before when he had been a hungry, homeless newsboy.

At the time of his death—April 13, 1936—Howard Thurston was the acknowledged dean of magicians, the king of legerdemain. During his last forty years he had traveled all over the world, time and again, creating illusions, mystifying audiences, and making people gasp with astonishment. More than sixty million people paid admissions to his show, and his profits were almost two million dollars.

Shortly before his death, I spent an evening with Thurston in the theatre, watching his act from the wings. Later we went up to his dressing room and he talked for hours about his exciting adventures. The plain, unvarnished truth about this magician's life was almost as astonishing as the illusions he created on the stage.

When he was a little boy, his father whipped him cruelly because he had driven a team of horses too fast. Blind with rage, he dashed out of the house, slammed the door, ran screaming down the street and disappeared. His mother and father never saw him or heard from him again for five years. They feared he was dead.

And he admitted that it was a wonder he wasn't killed; for he became a hobo, riding in box cars, begging, stealing, sleeping in barns and haystacks and deserted buildings. He was arrested dozens of times, chased, cursed, kicked, thrown off trains, and shot at.

He became a jockey and a gambler; at seventeen years of age, he found himself stranded in New York without a dollar, and without a friend. Then a significant thing happened. Drifting into a religious meeting, he heard an evangelist preach on the text, "There Is a Man in You."

Deeply moved, and stirred as he had never been stirred before in his life, he was convinced of his sins. So he walked up to the altar and with tears rolling down his cheeks, was converted. Two weeks later, this erstwhile hobo was out preaching on a street corner in Chinatown.

He was happier than he had ever been before, so he decided to become an evangelist, enrolled in the Moody Bible School at Northfield, Massachusetts, and worked as a janitor to pay for his board and room.

He was eighteen years old then, and up to that time, he had never gone to school more than six months in his life. He had learned to read by looking out of box car doors at signs along the railway and asking other tramps what they meant. He couldn't write or figure or spell. So he went to his classes in the Bible School and studied Greek and biology in the daytime, and studied reading and writing and arithmetic at night.

He finally decided to become a medical missionary and was on his way to attend the University of Pennsylvania when a little thing happened that changed the entire course of his life.

On his way from Massachusetts to Philadelphia, he had to change trains at Albany. While waiting for his train, he drifted into a theatre and watched Alexander Herrmann perform tricks of magic that kept the audience popeyed with wonder. Thurston had always been interested in magic. He had always tried to do card tricks. He longed to talk to his idol, his hero, Herrmann the Great Magician. He went to the hotel and got a room next to Herrmann's; he listened at the key-hole and walked up and down the corridor, trying to summon up enough courage to knock, but he couldn't.

The next morning he followed the famous magician to the railway station, and stood admiring him with silent awe. The magician was going to Syracuse. Thurston was going to New York—at least he thought he was. He intended to ask for a ticket to New York; but by mistake he too asked for a ticket to Syracuse.

That mistake altered his destiny. That mistake made him a magician instead of a medical missionary.

At the floodtide of his fame, Thurston got almost a thousand dollars a day for his show. But I often heard him say that the happiest days of his life were when he was getting a dollar a day for doing card tricks for a medicine show. His name was painted in blazing red letters across a streaming banner, and he was billed as "Thurston, the Magician of the North." He was from Columbus, Ohio; but that is North, if you are from Texas.

Thurston admitted that there were many people who knew as much about magic as he did. What, then, was the secret of his success?

His success was due to at least two things. First, he had the ability to put his personality across the footlights. He was a master showman, he knew human nature; and he said those qualities were just as important for a magician as a knowledge of magic. Everything he did, even the intonations of his voice and the lifting of an eyebrow, had been carefully rehearsed in advance, and his actions had been timed to split seconds.

And second, he loved his audience. Before the curtain went up, he stood in the wings, jumping up and down to shake himself wide awake . . . and he kept saying: "I love my audience. I love to entertain them. I've got a grand job. I'm so happy. I'm so happy!"

He knew that if he wasn't happy, no one else would be.

TWO-CENT NEWSPAPERS BOUGHT HIM CASTLES IN SPAIN, CUCKOO CLOCKS, AND EGYPTIAN MUMMIES

HAVE you ever wondered what you would do if you had a million dollars? William Randolph Hearst has an income of a million dollars a month—or thirty thousand dollars a day. During the time it will take you to peruse this short chapter, his income will mount by approximately one hundred dollars.

No one ever calls William Randolph Hearst, William. Even his most intimate friends call him "W. R.," and his seventy thousand employees always speak of him as "The Chief."

Millions of people read his twenty-four newspapers and nine magazines. He is the richest and most powerful publisher in the world. His name is a household word all over America; yet he himself is a man of mystery. The average person knows more about the private life of Mahatma Gandhi than he does about William Randolph Hearst.

The most astonishing thing I know about the most aggressive publisher in America is that he is reticent and shy. For half a century, he has been hobnobbing with celebrities; yet he actually dislikes being introduced to strangers.

27

WILLIAM RANDOLPH HEARST

$40,000. to move a tree—$500. to set a guinea pig's leg

He usually has anywhere from ten to sixty guests staying on his vast estate in California; but his favorite form of recreation is to steal away by himself and play solitaire. And when he is in New York, his favorite recreation is to go window shopping!

The most magnificent estate in the Western world is Hearst's ranch in California. It contains a quarter of a million acres of land and stretches for fifty miles along the rockbound coast of the ocean.

High on a wind-swept spot two thousand feet above the roar of the Pacific, he has erected a lordly group of Moorish Castles which he calls "The Enchanted Hill." He has lavished uncounted millions of dollars in furnishing these castles. The walls are adorned with Gobelin tapestries that once beautified the chateaux of France. The hushed halls are glorified by soft paintings from the brush of Rembrandt, Rubens and Raphael, canvasses that are immortal. His guests dine in a huge banquet hall surrounded by priceless objects of art; but at lunch, they are given paper napkins.

He has a collection of wild animals that would make Barnum's circus look like a side-show. Herds of zebras, buffaloes, giraffes and kangaroos roam over the hills; thousands of exotic birds dart among the trees; and lions and tigers roar and snarl in his private zoo.

A friend of mine, Frank Mason, used to buy antiques for Hearst in France. Hearst purchases entire shiploads of art treasures—even entire castles—and brings them to America in packing boxes with every stone and brick and piece of timber numbered and labeled to show where it belongs so he can erect the buildings here with exact fidelity.

He purchased so many objects of art that he finally had to buy a huge warehouse in New York to store the things he isn't using. This warehouse has twenty employees, it costs sixty thousand dollars a year to keep it going, and it contains everything from cuckoo clocks to Egyptian mummies.

William Randolph Hearst's father was a Missouri farmer. He headed west during the gold rush of forty-nine, walked two thousand miles across the plains beside a team of oxen and a covered wagon, fought Indians, discovered gold and made millions. As he grew older, he loved to sit in the shade of a big tree on his estate. A few years ago, his son, William Randolph Hearst, noticed that this tree was blocking the view of the ocean from one of his windows. He couldn't bear to think of destroying a tree his father had loved, so he paid $40,000. to have the tree moved thirty feet.

He is very fond of animals. For example, one day a group of motion picture executives flew up from Hollywood to hold a conference with Mr. Hearst, but he kept them waiting while he comforted a pet lizard that had lost a part of its tail. On another occasion, he sent his private yacht for a doctor at midnight and paid a medical fee of $500. because a pet guinea pig had broken its leg.

Hearst is over seventy, yet he plays a fast game of tennis. He has been playing tennis for forty years, but he is still taking lessons to improve his game. He is an expert amateur photographer, and takes thousands of pictures every year. He is also an expert shot with a rifle. One day while out on his yacht, he surprised his guests by holding his revolver at his hip, firing at a sea gull, and bringing him down on the wing.

He is an expert clog-dancer, an excellent mimic, and a good story-teller. His memory is almost like an encyclopedia. For example, if you asked him to name the wives of Henry the Eighth, or to call off the presidents of the

United States, the chances are a hundred to one that he could do it without a hitch.

One day Jimmie Walker and Charlie Chaplin were visiting at Hearst's ranch, and they got into an argument over the exact phraseology of a certain quotation from the Bible; Hearst settled the argument by repeating the quotation word for word.

He loves to surround himself with young people; and he never permits anyone to mention death in his presence.

Hearst inherited thirty million dollars from his father. He could have led the life of an idler; but instead, he has worked from eight to fifteen hours a day for fifty years; and he vows he will never retire until God retires him.

LIONEL BARRYMORE

When he was hungry, he pawned his best friend's gold
tooth; when he was cold, he slept under a heap of books

I WAS there that night in 1918 when Lionel Barrymore opened on Broadway as Milt Shanks in *The Copperhead*. It was a brilliant occasion, a triumph that made dramatic history. An excited audience leaped to its feet and cheered wildly and frantically through fifteen curtain calls.

Fifteen years later, I had a long talk with Lionel Barrymore in the Green Room at Metro-Goldwyn-Mayer's headquarters on Broadway. When he began talking about his struggles for recognition as an actor, I was astonished. "What? You? A Barrymore, with all the prestige and glamor of your family behind you—surely you never had to struggle!" I demanded.

He looked at me a moment and, in his low rumbling voice, replied: "Why, there ain't no such animal as you're talking about. A famous name is often a handicap."

The Barrymore kids had a strange and rather haphazard childhood. Their father, Maurice Barrymore, was one of the most charming and captivating men who ever made off-stage history with his escapades.

He would spend his last nickel to buy an animal. He used to ship bears home—bears and monkeys and wild cats and a wide assortment of dogs. John and Lionel spent one summer in a farm house on Staten Island with

33

no one for company but an old negro servant and thirty-five dogs of all shapes, sizes and breeds.

When Lionel, Jack and Ethel Barrymore appeared in *Rasputin and the Empress*, Hollywood proudly announced that this was the first time they had all played together. But Hollywood was wrong. The three Barrymores made their debut together more than forty years ago. The theatre was a dilapidated barn in the rear of an actor's boarding house on Staten Island, and the audience was made up of kids from the neighborhood. Admission was a penny and the total box office receipts was thirty-seven cents. They played *Camille*. Ethel was the business manager and she paid Lionel and Jack ten cents each, and to their intense disgust, pocketed the remaining seventeen cents.

Neither Lionel nor John aspired to be stage stars. They both wanted to be artists, and Lionel studied art in Paris for a time.

I asked him if he was ever broke and hungry then, and he said, "Yes, lots of times, because I couldn't sell my sketches to the magazines. Of course, I could always get money by wiring home, but sometimes I didn't have enough money to send a wire. Jack and I had a studio down in Greenwich Village, too," he continued, "but we didn't have any money to buy furniture. In fact, we didn't even have a bed. So we slept on the floor; and when it got too cold, we covered ourselves with the books. There was another chap, a writer, living with us and he had a removable gold tooth; when we were broke, we pawned his tooth. I remember we tried every pawnshop on the East side, but we could never raise more than seventy cents on it."

At twenty-six, Lionel Barrymore was a star, with his name flashing in bright lights on Broadway. But at fifty-three, his fame was only a memory. While his handsome brother, John, was one of the highest-paid stars in the world, and his sister, Ethel, had a New York theatre named in her honor, Lionel was earning a quiet living out in Hollywood as a director.

His friends and family were shocked. They complained bitterly that the most talented dramatic actor in America was going to waste. But Lionel didn't complain.

He threw a skill and knowledge gained from thirty years behind the footlights, into directing pictures. He dreamed. He studied. He experimented. He was the first director ever to discover that the sound camera could be moved around the lot—a discovery that revolutionized talking pictures. He dazed the industry with such unforgetable films as Ruth Chatterton in *Madame X*, Lawrence Tibbett in *The Rogue Song* and Barbara Stanwyck in *Ten Cents a Dance*. He was fifty-three, and he honestly believed his acting days were over.

Just as he had resigned himself to directing for the rest of his career, he got his chance. Norma Shearer was making *A Free Soul*. A great actor was needed for the part of the father. Lionel Barrymore stepped in front of the camera and covered himself with glory. He won the medal of the Academy of Motion Picture Arts and Sciences. Then the very producers who had formerly regarded him as a "has-been" fought for his services. Hit followed upon hit—*The Yellow Ticket, Mata Hari, Grand Hotel, Rasputin and the Empress, Ah, Wilderness!*

I asked Lionel Barrymore if he was ever discouraged before he made his come-back in Hollywood. He replied, "No, I've been up and down all my life. Lots of people said I was through; but I never thought much about it. I was always too darn busy to worry about my troubles."

SOMERSET MAUGHAM

The sign against the Evil Eye is stamped on the bindings
of his books

THE PLAY THAT "WASN'T WORTH BOTHERING ABOUT" BECAME THE GREATEST DRAMA SINCE HAMLET

WHAT would you say is the greatest stage play ever written? When leading dramatic critics of New York voted, by secret ballot, on the ten greatest plays of all time, the first honors went to *Hamlet*, written more than three hundred years ago. And they decided that the second greatest play ever written was not *Macbeth* nor *King Lear* nor *The Merchant of Venice*, but *Rain*. Yes, *Rain*, that tempestuous drama of sex and religion, fighting tooth and claw, in the South Seas— the play based on a short story by Somerset Maugham.

Maugham has made $200,000. out of *Rain*. Yet he didn't spend even five minutes writing the play.

This is how it happened: He wrote a short story called *Sadie Thompson*. He didn't think much of the story— but one night, John Colton was staying at his house, and Colton wanted something to read till he fell asleep. Maugham handed him the proofs of *Sadie Thompson*.

Colton was fascinated with the story. It thrilled him. He got out of bed and paced the floor, and in his imagination that night he saw it as a play—a drama that was destined to become immortal.

The next morning he rushed to Somerset Maugham. "There's a great play in that story," he told him, "I've been thinking about it all night. Put me to sleep, eh? I didn't sleep a wink!"

But Maugham wasn't impressed. "A play?" he said in his crisp British voice, "Oh yes, possibly—a morbid sort of play. Might run six weeks. But it isn't really worth bothering about. Not really." And the play that he didn't think worth bothering about made him a fifth of a million dollars.

When the play was finished, several producers turned it down. They were positive it would fail. Then Sam Harris accepted it. He wanted it for a young actress named Jeanne Eagels. But the agent for the play objected. He wanted someone who was better known.

Finally Jeanne Eagels got the part and played *Sadie Thompson* with a passion and power that made her the sensation of Broadway. She played to packed houses for four hundred and fifteen rip-roaring performances.

Somerset Maugham has written many distinguished books such as *Of Human Bondage, The Moon and Sixpence*, and *The Painted Veil;* and he has written a score of successful dramas. But he didn't write his own most celebrated play.

Some people call him a genius now; but he was a financial failure for eleven years after he started writing. Think of it! This man who was destined to make a million dollars as an author earned only five hundred dollars a year for the first *eleven* years that he turned out stories and novels. Sometimes he went hungry. He tried to get a job writing editorials on a salary basis; but he couldn't. "I had to keep on writing," Maugham told me, "because I just literally couldn't hold down a job."

His friends told him he was a fool to keep on trying to write. He had already been graduated from medical college, so they urged him to forget fiction and practice medicine. But nothing could swerve him from his determination to write his name large across the pages of English literature.

Bob Ripley of *Believe It Or Not* fame, once said to me: "A man will work and slave in obscurity for ten years and then become famous in ten minutes." That is about what happened to both Ripley and Maugham.

Here is how Somerset Maugham got his first break. Somebody's play had failed in London, and the manager of the theatre was looking around for something to replace it. He wasn't looking for a hit—just any old thing would do to fill in until he could get a real play into rehearsal. So he fished around in his desk, and pulled out a play by Somerset Maugham. *Lady Frederick*, it was called. He had had it in his desk for a year; he had read it; it wasn't much of a play—he knew that. But it might do for a few weeks. He put it on—and the miracle happened. *Lady Frederick* was a smash hit. It set all London talking. It tickled England as nothing had since the sparkling dialogue of Oscar Wilde.

Immediately every theatre manager in London begged for a play by Somerset Maugham. He dug old manuscripts out of his desk; and within a few weeks, *three* of his plays were playing to capacity houses.

Royalties came pouring in in a golden flood. Publishers fell over each other bargaining for the work of this new genius. Society showered him with invitations; and after eleven years of oblivion, Somerset Maugham found himself the toast of Mayfair drawing rooms.

Maugham told me that he never writes after one o'clock. He says his brain goes dead in the afternoon. He writes in a penthouse on top of his Moorish villa on the French Riviera. He always smokes his pipe and reads philosophy for an hour before he starts to write.

He told me that he isn't superstitious—nevertheless he has the sign of the Evil Eye stamped on the bindings of his books. He has the same curious design on the family plate. He has it on his stationery, and on his playing cards. He has it carved on the mantel above the fireplace, and he even has it carved above the entrance to his villa. But when I asked him if he really believed in it, he merely smiled.

CINDERELLA DANCED HER WAY TO HOLLYWOOD—AND DIETED HER WAY TO BEAUTY!

A DOZEN years ago, a little college girl in Missouri used to cry herself to sleep at night. In those days, she cried because she was lonesome. But today, excited crowds surge about her whenever she appears in public, and her face and name are known by countless millions of people on every continent washed by the seven seas.

A dozen years ago, this girl waited on the tables at Stephens College in order to pay for her board; and she was so poor that she borrowed fifty cents now and then from the night watchman. She couldn't go out to a party even if she got an invitation, because she had nothing to wear but the cast-off clothing other girls had given her. Today she is one of the best-dressed women in Hollywood. Today her clothes are so smart, so chic, that she creates vogues, and her gowns are eagerly copied by women all over the world. Dressmakers beg her to make their fortunes by wearing one of their latest creations in public.

Who was this lonesome, miserable, unhappy little girl —so poor she couldn't afford to buy herself a dress? Her name was Lucille LeSueur. Never heard of her? Well, that's her real name; but in Hollywood, she is known as Joan Crawford.

41

Courtesy Metro-Goldwyn-Mayer

JOAN CRAWFORD
She broke her ankle, but kept right on dancing

Joan Crawford is the tops now. But she knows what it is to be stranded in a strange town without a dime. She knows what it is to be hungry and not have a nickel to buy food. She knows what it means to battle her way through years of heartache and unending struggle. As a child in Lawton, Oklahoma, Joan Crawford spent most of her time racing around the neighborhood playing marbles and skinning-the-cat with the boys. But the greatest thrill of all was acting. She and her playmates took some old empty boxes out to the barn and made a stage out of them. They lighted a lantern to give the effect of footlights; and there with the horses and pigeons and English sparrows for her audience, Joan Crawford began her amazing career.

She determined then and there that someday she would be an actress and a lady and wear fine clothes. She promised herself that when she grew up, she would wear a red velvet gown with gold slippers, and an enormous hat with ostrich plumes.

When Joan was eight years old, her mother moved to Kansas City, and put Joan in a convent in Kansas City where she had to work for her board. No more exciting races with the boys now. No more acting in the old barn. In return for her board, she had to help clean fourteen rooms, cook and wash dishes for twenty-five children, besides undressing them and putting them to bed. She wore blue and white calico dresses and slept in one of a long row of iron beds.

Six years later, she decided to take a flyer in higher education; so she enrolled as a student in Stephens College at Columbia, Missouri. Money? She didn't have any money. As I have already said, she wore the cast-off clothes that the other girls gave her and she worked as a waitress in order to get free board and room. Some of the girls who snubbed and high-hatted her in those days because she had to work as a waitress now say: "Joan Crawford? Oh, yes, I know her well. We are very dear friends. We used to go to college together."

Stephens College itself now shines in her reflected glory and a large picture of her hangs proudly on the dining room wall and underneath the picture is this inscription: "Joan Crawford used to wait on tables in this room."

Her burning ambition then was to become a dancer. So when she was offered a job dancing with a road show for twenty dollars a week, she grabbed it, and felt she was tiptoeing on the edge of paradise. Two weeks later, the show closed. There was no money to pay salaries, and she was left broke and stranded in a strange town.

Did that kill her determination to go on the stage? Never! She borrowed money, got back to Kansas City, worked, saved her pennies, and boarded a Sante Fé train one morning headed for Chicago. After paying for her ticket she had only two dollars left. She was afraid to spend that—so she missed a couple of meals that day.

She got a job dancing in a cabaret; then she came to New York and danced at the Winter Garden as a chorus girl. A movie scout for the M.G.M. studios saw her dance in *The Passing Show*. She had grace, rhythm, youth, personality and a beautiful pair of legs. He suggested that she take a screen test.

"What? The movies? Oh, no!" She aspired to be the Pavlova of Broadway. Finally, after much arguing, she condescended to take a screen test and was handed a ticket for Hollywood and a contract for seventy-five dollars per week. But Hollywood turned thumbs down on her name. Lucille LeSueur? Poetical—yes. But disastrous for a movie actress. Nobody could remember it or pronounce it. So a movie magazine staged a contest, offered prizes, and names came pouring in by the thousand in every mail. As a result of that contest, "Lucille LeSueur" became Joan Crawford.

But she was still far from being a star. She played bits, acted as an extra, doubled for Norma Shearer. And at night she danced; the Charleston, the Black Bottom, the St. Louis hop. She wore out dozens of pairs of shoes in contests—and won dozens of loving cups.

But she wasn't the Joan Crawford then that she is now. She was a rather plump little girl with a lot of frizzled hair and a hard-boiled manner that was supposed to cover up her shyness. Then one day she realized that if she was going to stay in Hollywood, she would have to change. Ambition made a different person of her overnight. She stopped dancing the nights away.

She settled down to a routine of hard, serious study: French, English and singing. She began to reduce, and for three years, she was constantly hungry. She rarely has anything for breakfast now except a glass of water flavored with a dash of orange juice. Often she touches nothing but a little buttermilk all day. She worked hard, and began to be given better parts. In one picture, when her role called for an apache dance, she fell and broke her ankle. But she was so afraid she would lose the part that she had the doctor tape up her leg and foot, and continued with the picture.

Joan Crawford says that she herself is astonished at what has happened to her. She was born in poverty and now has every luxury that wealth can buy.

She was born without position and she is now surrounded by mobs of admirers wherever she goes.

She was born without beauty—and is now one of the most beautiful women on the screen.

CLARENCE DARROW
He fought through seven courts for seven years for the
sake of a $5. harness

A SMALL-TOWN INSULT MADE HIM THE
GREATEST CRIMINAL LAWYER
OF HIS TIME

NEARLY three-quarters of a century ago, a school teacher boxed the ears of a little boy because he was restless and fidgety and squirming in his seat. She boxed his ears in front of the other pupils, and humiliated him so that he cried all the way home. He was only five years old at the time, but he felt that he had been treated with cruelty and injustice; he learned to hate cruelty and injustice with a hatred that has kept him fighting all his life.

That boy's name was Clarence Darrow, today probably the best-known lawyer in America—and certainly the greatest *criminal* lawyer of his time. His name has flashed time and again in bold headlines across every newspaper in the land. He is a crusader, a rebel, a fighter, a champion of the underdog.

The first case he ever handled is still talked about by the old-timers in Ashtabula, Ohio. The burning issue involved was nothing more vital than the ownership of a second-hand set of harness worth five dollars. But to Clarence Darrow there was a principle at stake. Injustice had raised its snarling head and he fought it as he would have fought a Bengal tiger. He was paid only five dollars to fight the case; but he fought it, at his own expense, through seven courts for seven years—and won it.

Darrow says he has never been ambitious for money or prestige. He says he has always been a lazy cuss. He started out in life teaching a country school. One day an incident happened which changed his whole career. There was a blacksmith in town who studied law when he wasn't busy shoeing horses. Clarence Darrow heard this blacksmith argue a law case in the tinsmith's shop. He was fascinated with the wit and eloquence of these country spellbinders. He loved a scrap himself; so he borrowed the blacksmith's law books and began to study law. On Monday morning, he would take his law books to school, and while his pupils were studying geography or arithmetic, he thumbed through the pages of his Blackstone.

He admits he might have remained a country lawyer all his days if something hadn't happened to goad him into action.

He and his wife decided to buy a small house in Ashtabula, Ohio, from a dentist. The price was thirty-five hundred dollars. Darrow drew five hundred dollars out of the bank (and that, by the way, was all he had in the world) and agreed to pay the rest in yearly installments. The deal was almost finished when the dentist's wife refused point-blank to sign the papers.

"See here, young man," she said scornfully, "I don't believe you'll ever earn thirty-five hundred dollars in *all your life.*"

Darrow was furious. He refused to live in such a town. So he shook the dust of Ashtabula off his feet and headed for Chicago.

His first year in Chicago he made only three hundred dollars—not even enough to pay his room rent. But the next year he made ten times that much—three thousand dollars—as a special attorney for the city.

"When my luck began to change," Darrow says, "everything seemed rapidly to come my way." Before long he was general attorney of the Chicago and Northwestern Railway Company, and well on his way to a big-money career. Then there was an explosion. A strike. Hatred! Riots! Bloodshed!

Darrow's sympathies were on the side of the strikers. When Eugene Debs, head of the railroad union was called to trial, Darrow threw up his job; and instead of defending the railroads, he defended the strikers. That was the first of Darrow's fiery, sensational trials—every one of them a milestone in courtroom history. Take, for example, the famous case of Leopold and Loeb, confessed murderers of little Bobby Franks. Public opinion was so shocked, so horrified, at the brutality of the crime that when Clarence Darrow undertook the defense of the two murderers, he was reviled and persecuted and called worse than a criminal for daring to defend the guilty boys. And why did he do it? "I went in," Darrow says, "to do what I could against the wave of hatred and malice. No client of mine has ever been put to death and if that should ever happen, I feel it would almost kill me. I have never been able to read the story of an execution. I always left town if possible on the day of a hanging. I am strongly against killing."

Society makes criminals, he says, and any man might be guilty of any crime.

Darrow himself has known what it is to face trial. He was once accused of bribing a jury, and had to use his powerful eloquence in his own defense. The most touching expression of gratitude he ever experienced was during his own trial. A former client of his met him and said, "Listen, you saved me from the gallows once when I was in trouble; and now you are in trouble and I'd like to help you out. I'll be glad to kill the chief witness against you, and it won't cost you a cent."

A few years ago, Darrow published a book, the story of his life; and I remember I stayed awake far into the night reading the chapter in which he outlined his philosophy of life.

"I am not sure of how much or how little I have really accomplished," he said. "I have blundered on my way and I have snatched as much enjoyment as possible from the stingy fates. Each day must be sufficient unto itself, keeping in view only the direction and the journey's end. I cannot realize that I am old. Where can the long day have gone? It has been only a short time since I started on the road with all the world before me and immeasurable time ahead for the journey I was to take: now the pilgrimage is almost over and the day is nearly done. How endless the unexplored road appeared to be and how short the foot-worn trail seems now."

STICK HIS HEAD IN A LION'S MOUTH?
—NOT WITHOUT A GAS-MASK!

H E HAS been clawed and chewed by tigers. He has felt a lion's teeth sink into his leg clear to the bone; elephants have mauled him; bears have trampled on him; he has been slashed by a black leopard and bitten by hyenas. He's been sent bleeding and torn to the hospital twenty-one times. And the last time, when Nero, the biggest of his lions, finished with him, he was in the hospital for ten weeks and nearly lost a leg.

Clyde Beatty has one of the most dangerous jobs in the world. He looks into the jaws of death, not once, but *twice* every day. The life insurance companies realize that he may be ripped to pieces by savage claws at any time; so they refuse to gamble on his life. He is the only performer in the circus who can't get an insurance policy.

He told me he had sometimes thought of quitting the lion and tiger business; but he says that if he had to punch a time-clock in a factory, or some similar job it would kill him. And if he's got to die, he'd rather be *gored* to death than *bored* to death.

Clyde Beatty has spent half his thrilling and exciting lifetime—fifteen years of it—under the big top. As a kid back in Chillicothe, Ohio, he was crazy about the circus.

One exciting day the Barnum and Bailey circus came to town. A laundryman stuck up a poster in his window.

CLYDE BEATTY

The life insurance companies say: "Not on *your* life!"

A glamorous picture in yellow and purple and red, showing a heroic lion trainer bravely cracking his whip over a cageful of roaring, snarling cats from Africa. Beatty rushed inside and begged the owner of the laundry to give him the poster after the circus left town. The laundryman said, "Yes, I'll give it to you if you'll run errands for me for a week." He agreed to this.

This twelve-year-old kid already had some roaring, snapping, snarling fiends of his own. Or at least, he made believe they were. He had five dogs which he had trained to sit up and beg, roll over, and walk around on their hind legs. And every so often he would stick up his circus poster and put on a wild animal act for the kids in the neighborhood. Every year after that, when the circus came to town, he went and begged for a job. But he was too young.

Then one summer when the big caravan chugged out of town, Clyde Beatty was aboard, his heart palpitating with excitement. For three days, his desperate parents searched for him frantically. His mother spent nights of weeping before a letter came saying he had a job cleaning out the cages with the circus. He was only fifteen and he was getting five dollars a month and a chance to live in Paradise.

In ten years' time, this youngster from Chillicothe, Ohio had outstripped every lion-trainer in history. He put on an act so daring, so fool-hardy, that even circus men themselves said it couldn't be done. And when they *saw* him actually do it, they said he was a lunatic and that his life wasn't worth a plugged nickel. He put forty snarling, spitting lions and tigers into the same cage, cracked his whip, and made them do their stuff. Forty lions and tigers bristling with hate and snarling with rage. No wonder the act created a sensation even among

circus people, for lions and tigers are mortal enemies—
they fight on sight. And on more than one occasion,
Beatty has found himself in a cage full of fighting, roaring, murderous jungle cats.

Yet strangely enough, Clyde Beatty says that lions
and tigers are *not* the most dangerous animals to control.
He's tried them all—lions and tigers, leopards, bears,
hyenas, and elephants. And he has found that the most
dangerous beast of all is the polar bear. And he says the
hardest trick of all is to make a tiger ride on an elephant's
back. In fact, he himself was nearly killed by an elephant
one day, just because he had been to the tiger cage, and
the elephant caught the hated scent of the tiger.

You've heard, haven't you, that animal trainers control
their animals by looking them straight in the eye? Clyde
Beatty told me that that is a lot of nonsense. The average
lion wouldn't give two hoots even if Mae West looked
him in the eye. He says the only reason he watches his
animal's eyes is to find out what they're up to and what
they're going to do next.

Beatty says no trainer has ever actually stuck his head
in a lion's mouth. It just looks that way. He says: "I've
known some pretty reckless animal trainers, but I have
never heard of one crazy enough to stick his head inside
the mouth of a lion." Besides, lions have halitosis so bad
that even their best friends would have to wear gas-
masks.

There's another popular idea—that lion-trainers use
red-hot pokers to control enraged animals. But Beatty
says that if you want to commit suicide, just enter the
cage of a lion or a tiger that has been burned with a red-
hot poker. His harmless weapons are a kitchen chair,
a whip, and a revolver filled with blank cartridges.

And if there's one thing that gets his goat, it's to be called a *lion-tamer*. He's not a lion-tamer, he's a *lion-trainer*. He says his lions are not tame—and neither are his tigers. In fact, they're just about as wild as they were when they snarled in the jungles of Asia or Africa.

Clyde Beatty says he's tried working with tame animals—animals born in captivity, and he prefers wild ones any time. Tame animals are just like spoiled children—they've been pampered and petted until they refuse to do anything.

The question he has been asked most often is this: can a lion lick a tiger, or will the tiger lick the lion? Frankly, he doesn't know. He's been in the big cage dozens of times with lions and tigers fighting all around him, but the lions always gang up and the tiger fights alone. When one lion starts fighting, all the lions in sight come to his aid—especially if the lions are brothers. Lions are just like boys—they can't see a scrap without mixing up in it. But a tiger has no race consciousness—he will sit up on his pedestal and actually yawn while some other tiger is being killed.

One of the most amusing stunts Clyde Beatty does in the Big Cage is to make a bear turn a complete somersault—the only trick of its kind in the world. He discovered it by accident. Beatty was in the cage one day when the bear came tearing at him, teeth bared, claws tense, and murder in his eye. This bear was out to kill, and his onslaught was so sudden, so fierce, that Beatty did the first thing that flashed to his mind. He hauled off and smashed the bear on the nose. Nothing else is so painful to a bear as a poke on the nose; and as Beatty's fist landed, the bear went over in a heap and turned a complete somersault. That's what gave Beatty the idea.

And today all he has to do to make that same bear turn a complete flip-flop, is to tap him gently on the nose with his whip.

Clyde Beatty knows the wild animals of the jungle and plain—knows them better than any other man living. Yet he says his favorite animal is the dog.

THE ILL-WIND THAT WRECKED A WHOLE TOWN—AND MAY YET SAVE THE WORLD FROM INSANITY

ONE of the most startling discoveries in the history of medicine might never have been made if a tornado hadn't wrecked a town in Minnesota a little over a half a century ago.

The town the tornado struck was Rochester, now world-famous as the home of the Mayo Brothers, two of the greatest surgeons living. And the discovery, which Doctor C. H. Mayo is still working on, is a drug to cure insanity. This drug is injected into the body of a feeble-minded or insane person, and presto! the circulation of the blood is changed and the person is restored to sanity.

What will this discovery mean to humanity? Well, here are some facts. Figure it out for yourself.

There are more patients suffering from mental diseases in the hospitals in the United States than from all other diseases combined. One student out of every sixteen in our high schools today will spend part of his life in an insane asylum. If you are fifteen years of age and residing in New York State, the chances are one out of twenty that you will be confined in an institution for the mentally ill for seven years of your life. During the last decade, mental diseases have almost doubled in the United States. If this appalling rate of increase continues

THE MAYO BROTHERS
Two small-town boys who became the greatest surgeons
in the world

for another century, half the entire population of the United States will be in the insane asylums and the other half will be outside trying to support them by taxes.

The Mayo Brothers, who are working on this amazing remedy, are among the most celebrated surgeons in the world. Physicians from Paris, London, Berlin, Rome, Leningrad and Tokyo journey to Rochester, Minnesota, to sit at their feet and learn. Sixty thousand patients a year, most of them facing their last chance against death, make pilgrimages to the Mayo clinic as to a Holy Shrine.

Yet, to repeat—if a tornado hadn't twisted and roared through the middle west fifty-two years ago, the world would probably never have heard of the Mayo Brothers or Rochester, Minnesota, or this cure for insanity.

When Doctor Mayo—the father of the Mayo Brothers —settled there seventy years ago, Rochester had only two thousand people. His first two patients were a sick cow and a sick horse.

When the Indian wars broke out, Doctor Mayo grabbed his musket and made the Redskins bite the dust. When the smoke of battle cleared away, he picked his way over the battle ground laying out the dead and treating the wounded. His regular patients were scattered for fifty miles over the prairies of Minnesota. Many of them lived in houses made of prairie sod. They couldn't afford to pay a physician, but good old Doctor Mayo sometimes traveled all night to allay their aches and pains. Sometimes he fought his way through snow storms and blizzards so blinding that he couldn't see his hand before him in broad daylight.

He had two sons, William and Charles, now famous throughout the world as the Mayo Brothers.

They worked in a local drugstore, learned how to fill prescriptions and pound up pills, went to medical college—and then a tragedy occurred, a tragedy destined to affect the history of medicine.

The tragedy was this: a cyclone, a tornado, swept over the prairies of Minnesota like an angry god. It blasted, it demolished, it smashed to smithereens everything in the path of its fury. It struck Rochester and knocked it into a cocked hat. Hundreds of people were wounded and twenty-three were killed. For days, the Mayo Brothers and their father worked among the ruins, bandaging wounds, setting broken limbs, and performing operations. Sister Alfred, Mother Superior of the Convent Sisters of St. Francis, was so impressed with their work that she offered to build a hospital if the Mayos would take charge of it. They agreed, and when the Mayo clinic was opened in 1889, old Doctor Mayo was a man of seventy and his two sons had never even served as hospital internes. "We were the greenest of a green crew" —that is the way they describe themselves. Yet today William Mayo, the older brother, is considered the world's greatest authority on cancer. Each brother believes the other is the greater man—and both are famous for the cleanest work that surgery has every known. They work surely and swiftly—work with a swiftness that astonishes most surgeons. Arriving at the clinic at seven in the morning, they operate constantly for four hours every day. They have been performing from fifteen to thirty operations a day for years. And yet they both continue to study, still try to improve their work —and they admit that they have much to learn. The entire city of Rochester now exists by and for the Mayo clinic. No street cars are allowed. The buses run silently and even the conversation in the streets is hushed.

Paupers and bank presidents, farmers and movie stars all have to take their turns in the waiting room, and all are treated alike. The rich pay according to their means, but no one has ever been turned away because he was unable to pay.

One third of the Mayo Brothers' work is charity. They have never sued for bills, they never take notes, and they never permit a man to mortgage his home in order to pay them. They take in cash whatever a man can afford to pay at the time and let it go at that, and they never ask a man how much he can afford to pay before they perform the operation.

One man mortgaged his farm to pay them for saving his life; and when they discovered what he had done, they returned his check and sent him a check of their own for several hundred dollars to compensate him for the loss he had sustained in his illness.

They are glorious examples of two small town boys who were never interested in making money; and yet it poured in upon them in a golden flood.

They didn't care for fame; yet they are the most famous surgeons in the United States today.

Their sole desire has been to aid suffering humanity. Over the desk in their waiting room is a framed inscription which explains the eternal truth of their success. That sign reads: "Have something the world wants and though you dwell in the midst of a forest, it will wear a beaten pathway to your door."

EDDIE RICKENBACKER

He has driven hundreds of thousands of miles, but never
had a license

CHISELING TOMBSTONES WAS TOO DANGEROUS FOR HIM—SO HE JOINED THE FLYING SQUADRON

THIS is the story of a man who apparently can't get killed, a man who defied disaster and flirted with death for a quarter of a century. He has zoomed down the track at hair-raising speed in more than two hundred automobile races; and in the bloody days of 1918, he shot down twenty-six German planes from mid-air—shot them down while explosive bullets whined and cracked within inches of his head; yet he never suffered a scratch.

Yes, this is the story of Eddie Rickenbacker, commander of the famous "Hat-in-the-Ring" Squadron, and America's Ace of Aces in the World War.

Immediately after the war, I was the manager of one of the most charming men I have ever known—Sir Ross Smith, the famous Australian Ace, the first man who ever flew above the Holy City of Jerusalem and the first man who ever flew half-way around the earth. I found Sir Ross Smith and Eddie Rickenbacker, both distinguished fighters and flyers, to be very much alike—extremely quiet and modest and soft-spoken, not at all like the men one expects to find behind barking machine guns, spitting death from the skies.

Up to the time he was twelve years old, Eddie Rickenbacker was a wild, undisciplined boy with a fiery temper, the leader of a neighborhood gang, busting street lights and raising cain in general. Then a tragedy happened. His father died, and overnight, little Eddie was changed into an old man. That is the way he expresses it.

The day his father was buried, he resolved to become the head of the family. So he quit school and got a job working in a glass factory for five cents an hour, and he worked twelve hours a day. He walked seven miles to the factory each morning, and seven miles home again at night to save ten cents' carfare. The boy was determined to forge ahead. Nothing could stop him. The work in the glass factory was monotonous, dull, deadly. He despised it. He longed to be an artist, to create, to dream dreams in color and lines. So, he studied drawing in a night school and got a job chiseling angels and cherubs in marble for a man who sold tombstones. He chiseled the inscription on the stone that now stands above his father's grave. But chiseling tombstones was dangerous work, he was told—the dust from the marble would get into his lungs. "I didn't want to die young," Eddie says. "So I started looking for something safer to do."

He was fourteen years old when he stood on a sidewalk one fateful morning and stared at the first automobile he had ever seen—a curious, weird contraption chugging and sputtering through the streets of Columbus, Ohio. Yet to him it was Destiny on Wheels. It altered his entire life.

Before his fifteenth birthday, he had landed a job in a garage; and he learned to drive by backing cars back and forth in a wooden building that had once been a livery stable. Building a workshop in his backyard, he made his own tools and was preparing to make his own automobile. Presently, an automobile factory started in

Columbus, and Sunday after Sunday, Rickenbacker went there and begged for a job. But Sunday after Sunday he was turned away. After he had been turned down for the eighteenth time, he turned to the astonished owner of the factory and said: "Look here. You may not know it, but you have a new employee. I am going to work here tomorrow morning. The floor is dirty. I am going to sweep it and run errands and sharpen your tools."

Salary? He didn't give two whoops about salary. He wanted a chance to get started, and he got it. Enrolling in a correspondence course in engineering, he prepared himself for the opportunities that lay ahead.

From that time on his rise was rapid—workman, foreman, assistant engineer, trouble man, salesman, branch manager.

Then the lust for speed, the craving for adventure, got into his blood. The glamor, the applause, the excitement of a racing driver captured his heart. He knew he would have to change. So he set about resolutely to conquer his fiery temper. He developed self-control. He forced himself to smile until his smile became famous.

The grueling grind of racing called for nerves, iron nerves. He knew that. So he gave up smoking and drinking and went to bed every night at ten o'clock. By the time he was twenty-five, Eddie Rickenbacker was one of the most famous racing drivers that ever roared around a track.

And here is a funny thing! He has driven cars hundreds of thousands of miles during the past thirty years, yet he has never had a drivers' license, and he doesn't have one even now.

And he doesn't believe in good luck charms. His friends used to give him rabbits' feet and tiny horseshoes and good-luck elephants; but one day while he was crossing the continent, he raised a train window and dumped all his good luck charms out on to the plains of Kansas.

When America entered the War, Eddie Rickenbacker was the idol of the automobile world; so he sailed for France as General Pershing's chauffeur. But driving a General about was too tame for his adventurous blood. He craved action, and he got it. He was given wings and a machine gun and within eighteen months, he had written his name at the very top of the list of America's War heroes and was smothered with decorations from three governments.

In a swiftly moving book of 370 pages, he has set down the epic story of his fights and flights. If you want to read a book that is packed with courage and action and hair-breadth escapes, go to your public library and ask for *Fighting the Flying Circus*, by Eddie Rickenbacker. It is the most thrilling chapter in America's air history.

THE FIRST RACER ON EARTH TO TRAVEL
300 MILES AN HOUR—HUNTS PIRATE
TREASURE FOR A THRILL!

WRITING of Eddie Rickenbacker reminds me of Sir Malcolm Campbell—for at a dinner one night I found myself seated between these two, both quiet and soft-spoken men, yet both itching with this unquenchable mania for speed!

I knew Rickenbacker went into the desperate game of racing in the first place because he needed money. But what about Campbell? Campbell is independently wealthy—I knew he didn't care if he never made another dime.

What was it? Fame? Glory? But he said, No—he just did it for the fun of it!

Then, turning to Eddie Rickenbacker, I asked him how he enjoyed watching Sir Malcolm zoom over the ground at a speed just a trifle too slow for a comet; and Rickenbacker, veteran of two hundred automobile races himself, handed me a jolt by saying: "I've never seen him. And I never intend to. I figure that every time he races, the chances of his being killed are four out of five!"

No other living creature had, at the time of our interview, ever hurtled over the earth's surface as fast as Sir Malcolm Campbell—three hundred miles an hour,

SIR MALCOLM CAMPBELL

Faster than wild fire—even in a jungle

five miles a minute, New York to San Francisco in ten hours! Four other men, it's true, had traveled faster than two hundred miles an hour—Segrave, Lockhart, Keech and Bible—and each one died a horrible death. Campbell is the only one left.

But he's a fatalist. Never worries. Never gets nervous. And when it's all over, he steps out of the car as calm as some fellow who has just driven home from the office.

When Campbell was sixteen years old, he told his father that he wanted to be a bicycle racer. His father threw up his hands in horror and immediately got his son a job as a clerk with Lloyds', the famous insurance company in London.

Sir Malcolm told me he worked in the office for two years and never got paid a cent. The third year they consented to give him a little salary. Today he is one of the directors of that world-famous firm.

He was only nineteen years old when he got the idea of selling libel insurance to English newspapers. The libel laws in England are much more severe than in America. Campbell soon had practically every newspaper in the kingdom signed up to a policy. And by the time he was twenty-one, he was independently wealthy. He immediately started buying motorcycles and automobiles and entering races. He has spent over fifty thousand pounds —a quarter of a million dollars—to satisfy his longing to break speed records.

And he has traveled thousands of miles looking for the perfect speedway on which to make his headlong dash at death. He has been to Denmark, the Sahara Desert, South Africa and Florida. But he told me that the finest racing track on earth is out in Utah—the salt bottoms of old lakes that dried up a hundred thousand years ago— salt that is hard and smooth as ice.

One time he was racing in Denmark, driving at one hundred and forty miles an hour, when—*Bang!*—one of his front tires shot off. It hurtled itself straight at the crowd standing along the roadway, killed a young boy, and then leaped clear over the crowd and bounced along a dizzy path for a whole mile before it came to a stop.

Sir Malcolm told me the greatest thrills he ever got were during the war. He was an aviator, flying planes out of England, across the Channel and over to the Western Front. He had to fly planes he had never been in before, and he had to land them at places he could hardly see and on fields he knew nothing about. Sometimes he had to fly over battlefields with German pilots diving at him out of the clouds and peppering him with machine-gun fire. Yet he did that for nearly four years and never got a scratch!

But Campbell's greatest adventure—and he has written a fascinating book about it—was on Cocos Island where he hunted for hidden treasure. Hidden pirate treasure! Cocos Island in one of the dreariest places on the face of the globe. There is not a single house there and you never see a human being. The natives are degenerate survivors of the one-time cultured and wealthy Incas. By day, they hide up in the hills. At night, when they steal down to the water's edge, they are quieter than the very shades of the green palm trees that fringe the beach. The white man's eye is not quick enough to spy them. Spiders, land crabs, centipedes and ants make the rocks and sand a seething, crawling mass. Flies and mosquitoes infest the air. Sharks tumble about in the surrounding water.

In order to find the treasure, Sir Malcolm Campbell had to follow a small stream and look for a big rock with a crack in it. A crowbar inserted in the crack would make the face of the rock open like a door. And there before him would be gold—pirate's gold—millions and millions of it and glittering jewels. The wealth of Aladdin.

Well, Campbell followed every little stream he could find. He even followed some that were dried up. He literally beat his way through the wild jungle and blasted rock after rock. All in vain.

One day while he was beating and hacking his way through the stinging grass and thick undergrowth, he noticed that the wind was blowing to the North. That was the direction he was traveling. So he and his companion decided to set a fire and burn a pathway before them. He lit a match. Instantly there was the crackle and snap of burning wood. In five minutes, the jungle was a red hot roaring furnace!

Suddenly, to their horror, they saw that the flames were leaping in all directions. The fire was roaring down upon them. They were in danger of being roasted alive. So they began a mad, wild, pell-mell dash through the jungle, racing against a horrible death.

Finally, gasping for breath, blackened by smoke and scorched by flame, they flung themselves on the beach. Hundreds of acres of jungle were on fire and the flames lit up the sky with a burning red glow. It grew so hot that for a while they thought they would be driven into the water where dozens of man-eating sharks were waiting for them. But the palm trees were so green and wet they would not burn. Their lives were saved.

After three tantalizing weeks of treasure-hunting, all Sir Malcolm Campbell had to show for his search for pirates' gold was a pair of bloody feet, torn fingernails and a blistered back. He looked more like a convict than a wealthy English gentleman. Tired, discouraged, and feverish, he was eager to go home. But he told me that he is going back to Cocos Island some day, and if there is any treasure there, he will get it.

"You know," he said in his quiet way, "I'd go half way around the world for a little adventure."

HE STEPPED OUTSIDE FOR A FIGHT—
WHILE HE WAS GONE HE BROKE
THE BANK AND WON $10,000!

IN THE year 1921, a hot-headed young man was swaggering along the boulevards of Paris. His pockets were almost empty, but his heart was filled with boiling rage. Why? Because he had been robbed of four million dollars. Or at least his family had. Years ago, his father, an American geologist and mining engineer, had gone to Russia, discovered an oil field, and amassed a huge fortune. Then, after the war, the Soviets had confiscated his property and left him penniless. His son had fled to Paris to save his life, and there he found himself in 1921, with only twenty dollars between him and hunger.

So he took a chance. He drifted into a gambling club and bet five dollars on the game of chemin de fer. While his card was being drawn, a Frenchman stepped on his toes. He flared up like a rocket, called the Frenchman a swine, and demanded that he apologize *toute suite!*

Did the Frenchman apologize? He did not! He was highly insulted, and challenged the young American to a duel. They didn't have swords or pistols, so they rushed out behind the club and tore into one another with their bare fists. A couple of black eyes, a bloody nose—and then they were parted.

When the arrogant young American came back to the

ELY CULBERTSON
Now the most famous bridge-player in the world, he
once begged hand-outs at kitchen doors

gambling table, he was speechless. He had broken the bank. His stake had won not only once but, while he was fighting, his winnings had kept on mounting by geometrical progression until his five dollars had been boosted into ten thousand.

That fight changed the whole course of his life—and it also affected several million Americans. How? Do you play bridge? Do you play the Culbertson system? Well, there would probably have been no Culbertson system if it hadn't been for that fist fight, for when Ely Culbertson walked into the gambling club, he intended to join the White Russian army, run his bayonet through a few Bolsheviks, and fight for the return of his property. But now with ten thousand dollars in his pocket, he forgot all about war, took the first ship to America, rushed to Washington, sued the Soviet Government for four million dollars and intended to become a novelist or a professor of economics.

That was in 1921. Culbertson was a miserable card player then. But now he takes in half a million dollars a year or ten thousand dollars a week out of the game of contract bridge. However, that's not all profit by a long shot. He spends thirty thousand dollars a year in merely answering the countless questions that are constantly fired at him by bridge fans from all over the world. His assistants answer every question without charge.

Culbertson, whose name is almost a synonym for contract bridge, was brought up by a pious Scotch Presbyterian father who taught him that all gambling was sinful and that cards were a sinister device of the devil.

A student of Karl Marx and Tolstoy, he has always been obsessed with radical ideas. Even when he was a school boy in Russia, he organized a secret Revolutionary Committee among his fellow students, and used his American passport to go to Switzerland and smuggle back forbidden copies of a Bolsheviki newspaper that Lenin was publishing in Geneva.

When he came to America in 1922, he tried to get a job teaching philosophy and sociology; but he couldn't.

Then he tried selling coal, and he failed at that.

Then he tried selling coffee, and he failed at that.

Finally, he gave private lessons in French literature to a group of Socialists in New York and acted as concert manager for his brother, who is a violinist.

It never occurred to him to try to teach bridge then. He was only a poor card player, but a very stubborn one. He asked so many questions and held so many post mortem examinations that no one wanted to play with him. He read books about bridge, but they didn't help much, so he started to write a book himself. As the years went by, he wrote five books about bridge, but they were worthless, and he knew it, so he tore up the manuscripts before they were ever put in type. The books that he has written since then have been translated into a dozen languages and almost a million copies have been sold. One of his books has even been put into Braille so that the blind can improve their bridge games.

Culbertson first came to America in 1910. His Russian mother sent him here then because she wanted him to study at Yale. But he failed in his entrance examinations —failed because he didn't know enough English.

Think of it! He was an American citizen. He knew American history backwards and forwards. He spoke Russian, German, French, Spanish and Italian; but he couldn't get by in English. So he turned his back on Yale, drifted up to Canada, and got a job acting as a time-keeper for a gang of laborers who were building a railroad. With fiery oratory, he told them they were being cheated and underpaid, and robbed by the company stores. He stirred up trouble, organized a strike; and got himself kicked out of the company's employ.

He then walked two hundred miles to the nearest town, and beat his way to the Pacific Coast, traveling with hoboes, stealing rides on freight trains and begging for food at kitchen doors.

It is quite probable that some of the women out west who now play the Culbertson system, have handed out sandwiches and hot coffee to Ely Culbertson at their back doors.

TOLSTOY

His teachers despaired of ever pounding anything into
his thick skull

HE WAS ASHAMED OF HAVING WRITTEN
TWO OF THE WORLD'S GREATEST
NOVELS

HERE is a life-story as incredible as any tale out of the Arabian Nights. It's the story of a prophet who died in our own time—in 1910, to be exact—and who was so venerated that for twenty years before he died an unbroken and unending stream of admirers made pilgrimage to his home in order to catch a glimpse of his face, hear the sound of his voice, or touch the hem of his garment.

Friends came and lived in his home for years at a time and took down in shorthand every word that he uttered, even in the most casual conversation, and described in minutest detail even the most trivial acts of his daily life. These records were then printed in huge volumes.

Nearly 23,000 books—not 2300, mind you, but 23,000 books—and 56,000 newspaper and magazine articles have been written about this man and his ideas; and his own writings fill 100 volumes—a gigantic amount of words for any man to have written.

The story of his life is as colorful as some of his own novels. He was born in a forty-two room mansion, surrounded by wealth, cradled in the luxury of the old Russian aristocracy; yet in the last part of his life he gave away all of his lands, stripped himself of all his worldly goods, and died without a dollar in a lonely Russian railway station, surrounded by peasants.

In his youth, he was a snob, walking with mincing steps and spending a small fortune in the tailor shops of Moscow; yet in his later life he dressed in the rough crude clothes of a Russian peasant, made his shoes with his own hands, tended his own bed, swept his own room and ate his simple food on a bare table from a wooden bowl with a wooden spoon.

In his youth he lived what he himself described as "a dirty, vicious life," drinking, duelling, committing every sin imaginable—even murder; but in later years he tried to follow literally the teachings of Jesus and became the most saintly influence in all of Holy Russia.

In the early years of his married life he and his wife were so happy that they actually got down on their knees and prayed to Almighty God to continue their heavenly bliss, their divine ecstasy. Yet later on they were tragically unhappy. He finally came to loathe the very sight of her, and his dying request was that his wife should not even be permitted to come into his presence.

In his youth, he failed in college and his private teachers despaired of ever pounding any sense whatever into his thick skull; yet thirty years later he wrote two of the greatest novels that the world has ever known, two novels that will live and endure throughout the centuries—*War and Peace*, and *Anna Karenina*.

Tolstoy is more famous today outside of Russia than all the Czars who ever ruled that dark and bloody empire. Yet did the writing of these great novels make him happy? For a while—yes. Then he became utterly ashamed of them, and devoted the remainder of his life to writing little pamphlets, preaching peace and love and the abolition of poverty. These booklets were printed in cheap editions and trundled about in carts and wheel-barrows and sold from door to door. In four short years 12,000,000 copies were distributed.

A few years ago it was my privilege to know Tolstoy's youngest daughter in Paris. She acted as his secretary during the last years of his life and she was with him when he died. She is living on a farm now near Newton Square, Pennsylvania, and I learned from her own lips many of these facts about Tolstoy. Since that time, she has written a book about her father, *The Tragedy of Tolstoy*.

Truly Tolstoy's life was a tragedy, and the cause of his tragedy was his marriage. His wife loved luxury, but he despised it. She craved fame and the plaudits of society, but these frivolous things meant nothing whatever to him. She longed for money and riches, but he believed that wealth and private property were a sin. She believed in ruling by force, but he believed in ruling by love.

And to make matters worse, she was consumed by a fierce and fiery jealousy. She detested his friends. She even drove her own daughter away from her home, and then rushed into Tolstoy's room and shot at the girl's picture with an air rifle.

For years she nagged and scolded and screamed and abused him and, as he said, turned his home into a veritable hell because he insisted on giving the people of Russia the right to publish his books freely without paying him royalty.

When he opposed her, she threw herself into fits of hysteria, rolling on the floor with a bottle of opium to her lips, swearing that she was going to kill herself and threatening to jump down the well.

The Tolstoys were married almost half a century; and sometimes she knelt at his knees and implored him to read to her the exquisite, poignant love passages that he had written about her in his diary forty-eight years previously, when they were both madly in love with each other. As he read of those beautiful happy days that were now gone forever, both of them wept bitterly.

Finally, when he was eighty-two years old, he was unable to endure the tragic unhappiness of his home any longer, so he fled from his wife on the night of October 21, 1910—fled into the cold and darkness, not knowing whither he was going.

Eleven days later he died of pneumonia in a railway station-house, saying, "God will arrange everything." His last words were, "To seek—always to seek."

THEY CAME AFTER HIM WITH GUNS
AND T.N.T.—BUT HE STILL
RAISES EASTER LILIES

WHO is the most powerful man in the world today?
Mussolini? Stalin? Hitler? That, of course, is a
matter of opinion. But one thing is certain. The most
powerful man in the world of *finance* is J. Pierpont
Morgan, Dictator of Wall Street, High Mogul of the
World of Stocks and Bonds.

Yet, as a person, he is almost totally unknown. It
would hardly be an exaggeration to call him a man of
mystery. He shuns publicity, and his hatred of photog-
raphers amounts to a phobia.

When angered, he is blunt to the point of indiscretion.
In fact, he is so outspoken he has been called "the most
undiplomatic man in America."

Six feet tall, with two hundred pounds of dauntless
physical courage, he is utterly without fear. For example,
one day a maniac forced his way into Morgan's house,
whipped out a gun, and threatened to shoot. Morgan
might have dodged through a nearby door, but he didn't.
Instead, he walked straight toward the gleaming pistol.
Instantly there was the crack of an explosion. Morgan
staggered. The bullet had plowed into his abdomen. He
staggered, but he kept on coming. He leaped upon the
madman, wrenched the pistol from his hand. Then

J. PIERPONT MORGAN
His is the House that jack built

Morgan collapsed and fell to the floor unconscious. He was rushed away to a hospital. Death had missed him by a fraction of an inch.

Nowadays, it is almost impossible for an ordinary mortal to approach the mighty King of Gold in his office at 23 Wall Street—that low, squat citadel of high finance which is known simply as "The Corner." The sight-seeing guides never fail to point out to tourists the scars on the face of that building—sole reminder today of that hideous disaster of 1916 that wiped out the lives of forty people, injured two hundred more, and destroyed two million dollars' worth of property.

It happened precisely at one minute past noon. Happy, carefree crowds were pouring out of a thousand offices and no one paid any attention to a decrepit old horse and wagon that stood opposite the Morgan citadel.

Suddenly there was a blinding sheet of saffron-green light. Then a blast—a terrific explosion—that rocked the mighty skyscrapers on their very foundations. A bomb had burst,—a bomb loaded with a hundred pounds of T.N.T. A hail of deadly shrapnel swept the street.

A thousand windows were splintered to bits, a storm of broken glass roared down to the pavement. Awnings twelve stories above the earth suddenly burst into flame.

Arms, legs, and even human heads were hurled through windows twenty and thirty feet above the sidewalk, and flung upon ledges.

Men maimed, bleeding, and dying ran shrieking through the street, only to fall headlong in death.

The sirens of fire engines and the screaming of ambulances added to the bedlam of panic and fear.

And when the chaos was cleared away, all that remained of the horse and wagon that had brought the bomb was a bit of a wheel, two horseshoes, and a few nuts and bolts.

But Morgan, at whom all this was aimed, was in Europe at the time. He determined to capture the criminals responsible for that dastardly deed—to capture them no matter what the cost.

A reward of fifty thousand dollars was offered. The New York police, Federal agents, Secret Service men, private detectives, started one of the biggest man-hunts in history. The search led all over the earth. Departing ships were watched—and so were the Canadian and Mexican borders. The underworld of New York and Chicago and a dozen other cities were combed for clues. A king's ransom was spent in the search; but it ended in futility. A score of years have passed since then—and the mystery still remains a mystery.

Two armed detectives now keep constant vigil in front of the Morgan offices; and the roof of his low building is covered with heavy iron screening to protect it from bombs which might be hurled from neighboring skyscrapers.

In the inner sanctum of that solid, unostentatious building stretch two rows of desks, one behind the other, like seats in a school-room. At these desks work the eighteen Morgan partners—and at the very back of them all, like a schoolmaster supervising a class at examination time, sits Morgan, the head of the firm.

No other private banking house in the history of the world has played so important a role in the feverish affairs of nations. Not even the Medicis of Florence or the Rothschilds of Europe have enjoyed such far-flung prestige. The Rothschild saved Europe from Napoleon; but Morgan, more than any other single financial force, made the Allies victorious in the bloodiest war this troubled earth has ever known.

In 1915, Morgan & Co. floated the hugest foreign loan ever dreamed of. Five hundred million dollars—half a billion—went across the seas to serve as the sinews of war. The Morgans became the purchasing agents in the United States for the whole Allied armies. They bought billions upon billions of dollars' worth of arms and supplies. In one month, they spent more money than ordinarily passes hands over the entire surface of the globe in a like amount of time.

J. P. Morgan is as much at home in the pea-soup fog of London as he is in the roar and soot of New York. For years, while his father was living, he was head of the English branch of Morgan & Co., and when he came back to Wall Street, he introduced the English custom of having tea in the afternoon.

Even today, he has a house in Grosvenor Square, London. He keeps this house equipped with a full staff of servants, so that he can drop in any time—even after months of absence—and find the table ready for dinner, a fire roaring up the chimney, and the covers of his bed turned down.

He is the greatest pillar of the Episcopal Church in America, yet he corresponds regularly with Pope Pius XI in Rome. And when he visits the Vatican, he and the Pope sit for hours discussing—what do you suppose? —rare manuscripts written in Coptic, the medieval language of Egypt.

Mr. Morgan's private library houses many illuminated manuscripts written by the old monks five hundred years before Columbus discovered America. He has priceless folios of Shakespeare and a copy of the Gutenberg

Bible. That one book alone is probably worth a fifth of a million dollars.

J. P. Morgan is famous for his knowledge of Shakespeare and the Bible; yet he dearly loves to settle down to a good detective story, even as you and I.

Like his father, who was known as Morgan the Magnificent, he is a great connoisseur of art. He has spent uncounted millions on paintings, sculpture, tapestries, porcelains, and jewelry. And when he sold some of his priceless paintings, the story was flung in headlines across the front pages of every paper in New York.

On each Christmas Eve, a unique ceremony takes place in the Morgan Library. The children and grandchildren, and a few intimate friends gather round and listen to the story of Scrooge as told in *A Christmas Carol*. The story is read not from a printed book, but from the original manuscript written in Dickens' own handwriting.

In spite of all his wealth, many of Morgan's pleasures are very simple. For example, he loves to put on an old hat and coat and walk while the rain beats and lashes his face.

He adored his wife, and since her death in 1925, he has kept her room exactly as she left it. She succumbed to that mysterious disease known as sleeping sickness, and all of Morgan's millions were powerless to save the woman he loved.

Extremely fond of flowers, she belonged to a garden club which required its members to cultivate a garden with their own hands. And even today, J. P. Morgan—one of the world's richest men—puts on his overalls and hoes the weeds and ties up the vines in the garden which once belonged to his wife.

HIS PEASANT MOTHER WENT BAREFOOT
TO PAY FOR HIS MUSIC LESSONS AND
HE BECAME THE GREATEST
SINGER IN THE WORLD

WHEN Enrico Caruso died in 1921, at the age of 48, entire nations were struck dumb with sorrow; for the most beautiful voice in the memory of living men was still and silent forever. Caruso was snatched away from life while the plaudits of the world were ringing in his ears. Exhausted from overwork, he caught a common cold, neglected it, and for six months battled valiantly with death while the world that loved him sang masses, and sent a million fervent prayers winging their way up towards the inscrutable gates of destiny.

Caruso's magical voice was not merely a gift from the gods, it was the reward of long years of exhausting work —of patient practice and unflagging determination.

In the beginning, his voice was so light and thin that one teacher told him: "You can't sing. You haven't any voice at all. It sounds like the wind in the shutters."

For years, his voice cracked on high notes, and his acting was so poor that he was actually hissed during a performance. Few men have ever drunk so deeply of the heady wine of success as the immortal Caruso; yet at the very high noon of his fame, when he remembered the ordeal of those early years, he would burst into tears.

Self-caricature—New York Public Library

ENRICO CARUSO

The audience didn't know his name so they yelled for
"that drunkard"!

His mother died when he was fifteen, and all his life he carried her portrait with him wherever he went. She had given birth to twenty-one children. Eighteen of them died in infancy. Only three of them lived. She was merely a peasant woman who had known little else but hardship and sorrow; yet somehow, she sensed that this one son was hallowed by the fire of genius, and no sacrifice was too great for her to make. Caruso used to say, "My mother went without shoes in order that I might sing." And he wept as he said it.

When he was only ten years old, his father took him out of school and put him to work in a factory. Every evening after work, Caruso studied music, but he was twenty-one years old before he was able to sing himself out of the factory.

In those days, he jumped at the chance to sing for his supper in a neighborhood café. He frequently hired himself out to warble serenades beneath some lady's window. While the lady's tone-deaf lover stood out boldly in the moonlight going through all the gestures of adoration, Caruso, hidden in the doorway, would pour forth his soul in tones as mellow and seductive as Apollo's.

Finally, when he got his first real chance to sing in opera, he was so nervous at rehearsal that his voice broke and splintered like falling glass. Again and again he tried, but every note was a disaster, at last he burst into tears and fled from the theatre.

When he actually made his debut in opera, he was tipsy. He was so tipsy that the audience drowned out his voice with hoots and catcalls. In those days, he was only an understudy. One evening the tenor who sang the leading role was suddenly taken ill. Caruso was absent. Messengers were sent dashing through the streets to find him. Finally he was discovered in a wine shop, about three sheets to the wind. He ran as fast as he could to the theatre. When he arrived there breathless with excitement, the heat of the stuffy dressing room and the wine of the grape were too much. Suddenly the whole world began to spin like a merry-go-round. And when Caruso walked on to the stage, pandemonium broke loose in the theatre.

At the end of that performance, he was fired. The next day he was so heartbroken, so desperate, that he made up his mind to commit suicide.

He had in his pocket only one lira—just enough to buy a bottle of wine. He had had no food all day. And just as he was drinking his wine and planning how to kill himself, the door flew open and in dashed a messenger—a messenger from the opera.

"Caruso!" he shouted. "Caruso, come! The people won't listen to that other tenor. They hissed him off the stage. They're shouting for you! For you!"

"For me!" Caruso cried. "That's silly. Why, they don't even know my name."

"Of course they don't know it," the messenger panted. "But they want you just the same. They're shouting for 'that drunkard'!"

When Enrico Caruso died, he was several times a millionaire. His phonograph records alone earned him over two million dollars. Yet he had been so seared by the poverty of his youth, that up to the end of his life he wrote down every expenditure in a little book. Regardless of whether he bought a priceless bit of old lace or carved ivory for his collections, or tipped a bellboy, he made a note of the exact amount.

He was haunted by all the superstitions of the Italian peasantry. To the day of his death, he feared the Evil Eye. He never crossed the ocean without first consulting an astrologer. He never walked under a ladder, or wore a new suit on Friday. And nothing could induce him to begin a journey or start a new undertaking on Tuesday or Friday.

He had a veritable mania for cleanliness, and he changed his clothing—everything from underwear to spats—whenever he came into the house.

He possessed the rarest and most valuable voice in the world, yet he smoked in his dressing-room while he was putting on his make-up. When people asked him if smoking wouldn't hurt his voice, he merely laughed. He scoffed at dieting; and at every performance, just before he stepped on to the stage, he took a nip of whiskey and soda to clear his throat.

He had left school when he was ten, and he practically never read a book. He said to his wife: "Why should I read? I study from life itself."

Instead of reading, he spent hours over his collection of stamps and rare coins. He had an extraordinary gift for caricature, and every week he contributed a cartoon to an Italian periodical.

For years he suffered from excruciating headaches that tortured his senses and made him scream from pain. As he grew older, his astonishing vitality began to wane. He spent more and more of his time in the quiet of his study and cared less and less for the plaudits of the throng. Finally he succumbed to a brooding melancholy and spent hours poring over his newspaper clippings, cutting them out and trimming them and pasting them in his book of memories.

He was born in Naples. But when he first tried to sing in his home town, the papers criticized him and the audience was cold, and unresponsive. Caruso was deeply hurt and never forgave them. In the heyday of his glory, he often went back to Naples, but he bitterly refused ever to sing there again.

Perhaps the greatest and happiest moment of his life was when he first held his daughter Gloria in his arms. He said over and over again that he was only waiting for the moment when she would be big enough to run down the corridor and open the door of his studio. And one day in Italy, as Caruso stood by his piano, that very thing happened. He caught the little girl up in his arms, and with tears in his eyes, he said to his wife: "Do you remember—I was just waiting for this moment to come?"

And within a week he was dead.

THE DEAF, DUMB AND BLIND GIRL WHO
WAS LIKENED TO NAPOLEON

MARK TWAIN once said: "The two most interesting characters of the nineteenth century are
Napoleon and Helen Keller." When Mark Twain said
that, Helen Keller was only fifteen years old. Today she
still remains one of the most interesting characters of
the twentieth century.

Helen Keller is totally blind; yet she has read far
more books than most people who can see. She has
probably read a hundred times as many books as the
average person, and she has written seven books herself.
She made a motion picture of her own life and acted in
it. She is totally deaf, yet she enjoys music far more than
many people who can hear.

For nine years of her life, she was deprived of the
power of speech; yet she has delivered lectures in every
state in the Union; for four years, she appeared as a
headliner in vaudeville; and she has travelled all over
Europe.

Helen Keller was born perfectly normal. For the first
year and a half of her life, she could see and hear like
other children and had even begun to talk. Then suddenly she was overwhelmed by catastrophe. She was
struck down by an illness which left her deaf, dumb and
blind at the age of nineteen months and blighted her
whole existence.

HELEN KELLER WITH ANNE MANSFIELD
SULLIVAN

The most remarkable teacher and the most astonishing
pupil in history

She began to grow up like a wild animal in the jungle. She smashed and destroyed every object that displeased her. She crammed her food into her mouth with both hands; and when anyone tried to correct her, she flung herself upon the floor and kicked and thrashed and tried to scream.

In utter despair, her parents sent her to the Perkins Institute for the Blind in Boston, pleading for a teacher. Then, like an angel of light, Anne Mansfield Sullivan came into her tragic life. Miss Sullivan was only twenty years old when she left the Perkins' Institute in Boston and undertook what seemed an impossible task—the task of educating a deaf, dumb and blind child. Her own life had been filled with tragic and heart-breaking poverty.

At the age of ten, Anne Sullivan had been sent with her little brother to live at the poorhouse in Tewksbury, Massachusetts. The poorhouse was so overcrowded that the two children slept in what was known as the "dead room"—the room where dead bodies were laid out to await burial. The little brother was sickly and after six months, he died. And Anne herself, when she was only fourteen years old, had become so nearly blind that she was sent to the Perkins' Institute to learn to read with her fingers. But she did not go blind. Not then. Her sight improved. It was only a half-century later, and shortly before her death, that the darkness finally closed in upon her.

I cannot possibly make clear in a few words the miracle Anne Sullivan wrought with Helen Keller; nor how in one short month, she succeeded in communicating with a child who lived in an utter darkness and a withering silence. That story has been told unforgettably in Helen Keller's own book, *The Story of My Life*. No one who has read that book can possibly help remembering the happiness of the little deaf, dumb and blind child on the day she first realized there was such a thing as human speech. "It would have been difficult," she says, "to find a happier child than I was as I lay in my crib at the close of that eventful day and lived over the joys it had brought me, and for the first time, longed for a new day to come."

When Helen Keller was twenty years old, her education had advanced so far that she entered Radcliffe College, and her teacher went with her. By that time, she could not only read and write as well as any other student at College, but she had even regained her power of speech. The first sentence she ever learned to say was "I am not dumb now." She said it over and over again, thrilled, elated at the miracle—"I am not dumb now."

Today she speaks like a person who has a slight foreign accent. She writes her books and magazine articles on a typewriter that types in Braille, or raised dots. And if she wants to make corrections in the margin, she pricks little holes in the paper with a hairpin.

She lives in Forest Hills, a part of New York City. I live only a few blocks from her home; and when I go out walking with my Boston bull pup, I sometimes see her strolling in her garden with her shepherd dog for a companion.

I have noticed that as she walks, she often talks to herself. But she doesn't move her lips as you and I do—she moves her fingers, and talks to herself in sign language. Her secretary told me that Miss Keller's sense of direction is no better than yours or mine. She often loses her way in her own home, and if the furniture is moved, she is at a complete loss. Many people expect her to have a sort of uncanny sixth sense because she is blind, yet scientific tests have shown that her sense of touch and taste and smell are just about like yours.

However, her sense of touch is so acute that she can understand what her friends are saying by placing her fingers lightly over their lips, and she enjoys music by putting her hands on the wood of a piano, or a violin; she even listens to the radio by feeling the vibrations of the cabinet. She enjoys singing by putting her fingers lightly on the throat of the singer, but she herself cannot sing or carry a tune.

If Helen Keller were to shake hands with you today and then meet you and shake hands again five years later, she would remember you by your handshake—whether you were angry or happy, disappointed or gay.

She rows a boat and swims and loves to gallop through the woods on horseback. She plays checkers and chess with a set made especially for her. She even plays solitaire with a deck of cards that has raised figures; and on rainy days, she often spends the time knitting or crocheting.

Most of us think that about the worst affliction in the world is to become blind. Yet Helen Keller says she doesn't mind being blind nearly so much as being deaf. In the utter darkness and silence which separates her from the world, the thing which she misses most is the friendly sound of the human voice.

MUSSOLINI

Like a gypsy, he consulted the cards before making his
"march on Rome"

HE USED TO KEEP BOMBS IN THE STOVE—
BUT HE WON'T RISK SLEEPING WITH
MOONLIGHT ON HIS FACE

MUSSOLINI boasts of the fact that as a child he was a holy terror in his neighborhood. Aggressive, belligerent, he was always in trouble. He frequently came home with a black eye and bloody nose, and sometimes with his head cut open by a rock. Yet when he went away to a boarding school, he was so soft that he wept from homesickness.

Mussolini's father was one of the fiercest international revolutionists of his day, and he named his son Benito Juarez, after one of the wildest revolutionists in Mexican history.

Mussolini was expelled from boarding school; and later on he was chased out of Switzerland and France because of his radical activities. He was thrown into jail eleven times.

He has always been a great reader. Once, when the police came to drag him off to jail, he said: "Please wait until I finish reading this chapter, and then I will go with you."

At various times in his life he has been a Socialist, a Communist, an Anarchist, and now a Fascist.

Naturally, he made enemies along the way—bitter enemies. Several people tried to assassinate him. His motto is "Live Dangerously"; and he has. He took fencing lessons and fought many duels. He used to work with a dagger and two pistols on his desk, and he usually had his bookcase half-full of bombs. His enemies had threatened to kill him—and he was prepared. Once, when the police raided his office in the autumn, he hurriedly placed the bombs in the stove, and the next week the office boy started to build a fire while the bombs were still there.

When Mussolini joined the army in 1915 as a private, he was already editor of a Socialist newspaper and a famous man. So he was offered a safe berth far behind the trenches to write a history of the regiment. "I didn't come here to write," he said with indignation. "I came here to fight."

A short while later, his body was cut and torn by shrapnel. He was wounded in forty-two places, the surface line of all his wounds, if put together, would have measured one yard in length.

Mussolini once said: "I don't want soldiers who fight from a sense of duty. I want men who fight because they *love* to fight." His heroes are Julius Caesar and Napoleon, and his gray coat, which he wears as commander of the militia, is an exact copy of one worn by Napoleon.

Mussolini was brought up in poverty. His father ran a blacksmith shop in the lower floor of the house. His mother taught a few pupils upstairs, and the family was so poor that his mother appealed to the government for help. But the government didn't even bother to answer the letter.

Mussolini couldn't read until he was fifteen years old. When he was sixteen, he used to sit in the cowshed reading the novels of Victor Hugo while the oxen chewed their hay.

At eighteen years of age, he worked as a common laborer for six cents an hour, roasted a few potatoes in the ashes of a fire and slept on a heap of straw. He was a station porter, a bricklayer, a butcher boy—but he was always getting fired. So he tramped through Switzerland begging for bread and sleeping under bridges, and the police arrested him for vagrancy.

Mussolini was never interested in money. Once when he was working for a Socialist newspaper, his wife urged him to ask for a raise in salary. "I'm not working for money," he told her, "I'm working for an ideal." When the newspaper offered to raise his salary, he refused it.

When he was hungry and penniless, he would buy a glass of milk and then go to his bare room, take out his violin and drown all thoughts of hunger by playing Beethoven's Ninth Symphony.

While editing his newspaper, he would often write feverishly all day long and far into the night and then sleep on top of his office desk. He ate the bread and salami his friends brought him, and didn't leave his office for days at a time.

As a child, Mussolini was deeply influenced by an old witch who sold good-luck charms and love-potions and quack medicines. She taught him to interpret dreams and forecast the future by looking at a deck of cards. Before his historic march on Rome, he laid his cards out on the table and studied them carefully—not once, but many times.

Here is a quotation from Sarfatti's biography of Mussolini. "Even today Mussolini has strange things to say about the moon, the influence of its cold light upon men and affairs and the danger of letting its rays shine on your face when you are sleeping; and he is an adept in interpreting dreams and omens and in telling fortunes by cards. He can explain too why oxen allow themselves to be led by women and why the front paws of a hare are so short, and can throw light upon many other such mysteries."

Mussolini is quite gray, but he will not allow the Italian newspapers to mention his age or play up the fact that he is a grandfather.

He is a fatalist. He believes he won't be killed until his time arrives; yet he has three hundred men guarding him, and every spot in his home and office—even the drain pipes—are searched every day for bombs.

He has no intimate friends. He likes to eat alone. He doesn't confide in anybody, not even his wife. He once said: "If my own father were to come back to this world, I wouldn't place my trust even in him."

He takes a lukewarm bath every morning. He says cold baths are bad for his nerves. He shaves himself in the morning in order to save time. Sometimes he has a barber shave him in the evening, but the barber is ordered not to talk.

He has a room filled with presents that have been sent to him from all over the world. He calls it his "Museum of Horrors."

Mussolini once said that during 1934 he granted audiences to 60,000 people—more than a thousand a week or 150 a day—and that he had almost two million papers laid before him by his secretary—all in one year.

He was deeply in love with his mother, and her death stunned him into temporary paralysis. He wears on his right hand today a little gold ring that used to belong to her. This ring was his mother's one piece of jewelry, and it was the only legacy she left him.

NEW YORK'S QUEEREST RICH FAMILY

THE most talked-of house in New York used to stand at the corner of Fifth Avenue and Thirty-ninth Street. For twenty years it was called "The House of Mystery." Detective stories, newspaper articles, plays, and even motion pictures were woven around its grim, brick walls. Fifty-thousand people passed its nailed-up front door every day for years; yet rarely did anyone ever see a sign of life behind its shuttered windows.

If you ever rode up Fifth Avenue on a sight-seeing bus, possibly the Wendel House was pointed out to you as the only home in the world where a yard worth a million dollars was maintained so that the poodle dog would have a place to play in.

The Wendels were one of New York's richest families. Their real estate holdings were once valued at a hundred million dollars. Yet they loved to cling to the past. A bachelor brother and his spinster sisters lived in a house that had been built when Abraham Lincoln was still an unknown prairie lawyer out in Illinois. I walked past that house when it was being razed, and saw workmen carrying out zinc bathtubs and marble wash-stands that had been in use ever since the days of slavery.

The Wendels used gas for lighting because they believed it was easier on the eyes than electricity. They had no use for radios, for dumb waiters, for elevators, or

JOHN GOTTLIEB WENDEL

He wore shoes with soles an inch thick to insulate him
against germs in the ground

automobiles. The only modern improvement in the house was a telephone; and that was installed only two days before the death of the last of the Wendels, so that the nurse could call a doctor.

The Wendel House was assessed at only six thousand dollars; yet the lawyer often pointed out to the family that it was costing them a thousand dollars a day to live in a six-thousand-dollar house. That was true because the land on which it stood was worth almost four million dollars, and the interest on that amount plus the assessments and taxes amounted to about a thousand dollars a day.

But in spite of all this wealth, the Wendel family lived in the past.

John Gottlieb Wendel died in 1914, up to the time of his death, he had all his suits of clothes copied exactly from a suit he had purchased at the end of the Civil War. The suit was kept in the same box in which it had been delivered forty years earlier, and he had eighteen copies of it made at one time. He wouldn't wear any fabric that had been dyed; so, when he wanted a black suit, he got the wool from a firm in Scotland which supplied him with wool shorn especially from black sheep.

He carried an umbrella, rain or shine, winter and summer.

He had one straw hat which he wore year after year until it literally fell apart, but at the beginning of each season, he had it varnished a bright, new, shiny black.

When he invited his friends to lunch, he wrote the invitations in Latin.

He believed that all manner of mysterious diseases were contracted through the feet; so he had the soles of his shoes made of gutta percha an inch thick to insulate him against the germs in the ground.

In his day, John Gottlieb Wendel was New York's biggest one-man landlord. He grew rich simply by sitting tight and letting the city grow up around him.

The Wendel sisters were violently opposed to drink; they once refused to sign a million-dollar lease until they were promised that the first-aid kit and the medicine cabinet to be used in the building wouldn't contain more than a pint of alcohol. In spite of that, after their death, ten thousand dollars' worth of rare wines, whiskies, and champagnes were found in their cellar. It had lain untouched so long that hundreds of bottles had turned to vinegar.

John Gottlieb Wendel had seven sisters, and he did all in his power to keep them from marrying. He feared that if they married and had children, the estate would be broken up. So he warned them that all men were after their money, and when suitors came to call on them, he frankly told them not to call again.

Only one of the sisters, Miss Rebecca, married; and she didn't marry until she was sixty years old. The others faded into a desolate old age and died without companions. The story of their wasted lives is a pitiful illustration of how little money, in itself, can mean.

Georgianna, the most spirited of the sisters, fought against her family's restrictions until she developed a persecution mania and had to be sent away. For twenty years, she was confined to an institution for the mentally ill, and, when she died, in 1930, most of her friends thought she had been dead for years. She was worth five million dollars, but it didn't bring her five cents' worth of happiness.

Another sister, Josephine, lived alone in one of the Wendel country houses surrounded by no one but servants. The pitiful part of it is that she dreamed that the house was filled with noisy, happy children, and used to talk and play with them. She imagined that people came to see her, and she used to have her servants set six places at the dinner table. As each course was served, she would change places, pretending that she was all of the guests in turn.

One by one, as the sisters died, the rooms they had occupied were locked and the shutters closed; until finally Miss Ella left open only her bedroom, her dining-room downstairs, and the large bare room upstairs where she and her sisters had passed their lonely school days. For years, she lived alone in that spooky, forty-room house with a few faithful old servants and her French poodle dog, Tobey.

Tobey slept in Ella's room in a little four-poster bed exactly like his mistress'. And Tobey ate his dog biscuits and pork chops in the dining-room at a special brass table spread with a velvet cloth.

When Ella Wendel died, she left millions of dollars to the Methodist church for missionary work; yet she herself had seldom gone to church.

She died believing she hadn't a living relative in the world; but within a year, presto, two thousand three hundred alleged relatives sprang up like mushrooms all over the earth.

Two hundred and ninety appeared in Tennessee alone, all clamoring for a share of her thirty-five-million-dollar estate. The German Consulate filed a blanket claim on behalf of four hundred German Wendels, and Czechoslovakia produced so many heirs that they had to be handled through the Foreign Office.

Two persons claimed to be children of John Wendel

through two different secret marriages, and one of them served a sentence in jail for forging a marriage certificate and a will.

John Gottlieb Wendel never made a will. He said he "didn't want any lawyer making money out of his property." Well, the joke was on him, for before the estate was settled, not only one lawyer, but two hundred and fifty lawyers, had collected fees out of the gold-rush for the Wendel millions.

"HE SOUGHT THE SECRETS OF THE POLE—
HE FOUND THE SECRETS OF GOD"

I KNOW of no story more heroic, more inspiring, or more tragic than that of Captain Robert Falcon Scott, the second man to reach the South Pole. The tale of how Scott and two companions met tragic death on the Ross Ice Barrier still has the power to sway mankind.

The news of Scott's death reached England on a sunny afternoon in February, 1913. Crocuses were blooming in Regent Park. England was stunned as nothing else has stunned her since Nelson's death at Trafalgar.

Twenty-two years later, England dedicated a final memorial to Scott—a polar museum, the first polar museum in the world. Arctic explorers from all over the earth gathered at its dedication. Across the front of the building runs a Latin inscription of Robert Scott. It says: "He sought the secrets of the Pole. He found the secrets of God."

Scott began his tragic dash for the South Pole in the *Terra Nova*, and from the moment the ship nosed her way into the icy waters of the Circle, he was beset and bedevilled by bad luck.

Enormous waves battered the hull. Cargo was swept from the deck. Tons of sea water thundered down into the hold. The boiler fires were swamped. The pumps were clogged. And for days the gallant ship rolled helplessly in the trough of the smashing seas.

CAPTAIN ROBERT FALCON SCOTT

His is one of the most heroic and tragic tales of all time

But Scott's bad luck had only begun.

He brought along tough little ponies that had been hardened to cold on the frozen tundras of Siberia, but they suffered agonies. They floundered helplessly in the powdery snow; they broke their legs in treacherous crevasses and had to be shot.

The dogs too—veteran huskies from the Yukon— went wild and dashed blindly over the edges of the glacier cracks.

Then Scott and his four companions made the final dash for the Pole, alone, harnessed to a sledge that weighed a thousand pounds. Day after day they slogged over fields of rough ice, each man pulling, gasping and choking in the thin frigid air nine thousand feet above sea level.

Yet they did not complain. At the end of the cruelest journey ever undertaken by man lay victory, lay the mysterious Pole, undisturbed since the Six Days of Crea- tion—the Pole where nothing lives nor breathes, nor stirs—not even a wandering gull.

And on the fourteenth day they reached the Pole— *but*—only to find consternation and heartbreak. Before them, at the top of a stick, a tattered piece of cloth flaunted triumphantly in the bitter wind. A flag—the flag of Norway! Amundsen, the Norwegian had been there before them!—and they realized that after years of preparation, after months of torment, they had been cheated of victory by five short weeks.

Crushed with disappointment they started home.

The story of their tragic struggle back toward civiliza- tion is an Odyssey of suffering. The stinging blasts coated their features with ice and froze their very beards. They stumbled and fell, and every injury brought them a step nearer death. First, Petty Officer Evans, the strongest man in the outfit, slipped and crashed his skull against the ice, and died.

Then Captain Oates fell ill. His feet were frostbitten. He could hardly walk. He knew he was holding his companions back. So one night Oates did a godlike thing. He walked out into a raging blizzard to die in order that others might live.

Without heroics, without melodrama, he calmly announced: "I'm going outside. I may be gone some time." He was gone forever. His frozen body was never found. But today a monument stands on the spot of his disappearance, and it reads: "Hereabouts died a very gallant gentleman."

Scott and his two companions staggered on. They no longer looked like men. Their noses, their fingers, their feet were brittle with cold. And on the nineteenth of February, 1912, fifty days after they had left the Pole, they pitched camp for the last time. They had fuel enough to make two cups of tea apiece, and enough food to keep them alive for two more days. They thought they were saved—they were only eleven miles away from a depot of buried supplies. With one terrible march they could make it.

Suddenly they were overwhelmed with tragedy.

Down over the rim of the earth roared a howling blizzard, a fury of wind so fierce, so sharp that it cut ridges in the ice. No creature on earth could face it and live. Scott and his men were held prisoners in their tent for eleven days while the blizzard raged and snarled. Their supplies were exhausted. It was the end and they knew it.

There was a way out—an easy way out. They had opium, a large quantity of opium brought along for just such an emergency. A big dose of that and they could all lie down to pleasant dreams, never to wake again.

But they ignored the drug. They resolved to face death with the fine sportsmanship characteristic of old England.

During the last hour of his life Scott wrote a letter to Sir James Barrie, describing the end. Their food was gone. Death was almost upon them. Yet Scott writes: "It would do your heart good if you could hear us fill our tent with ringing songs of cheer."

One day eight months later when the Antarctic sun shone peacefully over the gleaming ice, their frozen bodies were found by a searching party.

They were buried where they perished—buried under a cross made of two skiis lashed together. And over their common grave were written these beautiful words from Tennyson:

> *One equal temper of heroic hearts*
> *Made weak by time and fate but strong in will*
> *To strive, to seek, to find, but not to yield.*

EDWARD BOK

He knew nothing about women, but he told millions of
them how to live

HOW A FOURTEEN-YEAR-OLD IMMIGRANT BOY MET THE GREATEST MEN IN AMERICA

ONE day a hungry little boy coming home from school stopped before a bakery window to admire the hot buns and custard pies.

The baker stepped out and said to him:

"Look pretty good, don't they?"

"They would," replied the little Dutch boy, "if your window were clean."

"Why, that's so, too," said the baker. "Maybe you'll clean it for me."

And that was how Edward Bok got his first job. It paid him only fifty cents a week but it looked like a fortune; for his people were so poor that he used to go out in the street with a basket every day and collect stray bits of coal that had fallen in the gutter where the coal wagons had delivered fuel.

That boy, Edward Bok, had come to this country so utterly ignorant of English that he couldn't understand a word his teacher said to him and he never got more than six years' schooling in his life; yet he became one of the most successful magazine editors in the history of American journalism.

He admitted he was almost totally ignorant of what women like to read; yet he built up the greatest women's magazine in the world, and kept its circulation pyramiding and sky-rocketing until, in the month he retired, two million copies were sold, and one million dollars' worth of advertising appeared within the covers of a single issue.

Edward Bok was editor of the *Ladies' Home Journal* for thirty years; then he retired; and wrote the story of his life, called *The Americanization of Edward Bok*.

After washing windows for the bakery shop, Edward Bok began collecting jobs with the same gusto which most boys reserve for collecting stamps. On Saturday mornings, he ran a paper route; on Saturday afternoons and Sundays, he peddled ice water and lemonade to the thirsty passengers on the horse cars; and in the evenings, he began to write up birthday parties and pink teas for the local newspaper. Finally, he was averaging between sixteen and twenty dollars a week—all in his extra time after school. He was only twelve years old and he had been in America less than six years.

He was only thirteen when he left school to become an office boy for the Western Union; but he didn't for one moment give up the idea of an education. Instead, he started to educate himself. He saved his carfares and went without lunch until he had enough money to buy an encyclopedia of American biography—and then he did an unheard-of thing. He read the lives of famous men and wrote them asking for additional information about their childhoods. He wrote General James A. Garfield, who was then running for President, and asked if it was true that he was once a tow-boy on a canal. He wrote General Grant about a certain battle and Grant drew a map for him and invited this fourteen-year-old boy to have dinner with him and spend the whole evening talking to him.

By this same process, this boy who was working in a

telegraph office for six dollars and twenty-five cents a week, soon made the acquaintance of the most distinguished men of his day. He visited Emerson, Philip Brooks, Oliver Wendell Holmes, Longfellow, Mrs. Abraham Lincoln, Louisa May Alcott, General Sherman, and Jefferson.

Mingling with these distinguished people gave him a confidence, a vision and an ambition that were priceless.

One day he saw a man open a package of cigarettes on the street, take out a souvenir photograph and throw it away. Edward Bok was always on the look-out for new and famous people to write to—so he picked up the photograph and looked at it. It was a picture of a famous statesman, but the other side of the photograph was a complete blank. Bok thought: "If there had been a short biography of this famous man on the other side, probably this picture wouldn't have been thrown away."

That gave him an idea. The next day in his lunch hour he set out to find the company that published the photographs. He got hold of the man in charge and talked to him. He talked so eagerly and so convincingly that before he left, he had an order to supply a hundred such biographies at $10. apiece—or ten cents a word. Soon he was asked to supply so many that he couldn't possibly do all the work himself, so he had several reporters working for him, supplying him biographies at $5. apiece—or exactly one half the price he himself was getting.

Finally he threw up his telegraph job entirely and tackled the publishing field in earnest.

He was just twenty-six years old when he went to Philadelphia to take charge of the *Ladies' Home Journal*; and he was just fifty-six—in the prime of life—when he closed his desk for the last time and said "I'm through."

In those thirty years, he had created for himself a

unique place in American journalism. Of course, he had made a fortune; but a man's success isn't measured in money alone. Let's see, for example, what Edward Bok did for you personally.

Well, to begin with, the food you eat is probably purer and more wholesome because of his fight for pure food laws. The city you live in is doubtless cleaner and more sanitary because he waged a relentless campaign against dirty and unsightly city dumps. The house you live in is probably more beautifully built and more tastefully furnished because of his unremitting crusade against the stuffiness and ugliness of the late Victorian era. In those days, house designs were as ugly as they were ornate, and as expensive as they were horrible. Edward Bok was the first man to recruit the best architects in the country to supply house plans so cheaply that anyone could afford them. And he succeeded so well that Theodore Roosevelt once said of him: "Edward Bok is the only man I ever heard of who changed, for the better, the architecture of *an entire nation.*"

In the ten years of life that were left to him after his retirement, he began to build gardens. He imported tens of thousands of bulbs from his native Holland and planted them by road sides to delight the public eye . . . he turned railroad stations into flowering embankments of roses . . .

But his most famous and most lasting monument is the wonderful Singing Tower in Florida. What was once only a bare stretch of sand on the highest elevation in Florida is now a bird sanctuary, a verdant grove of hundreds of thousands of green trees and shrubs; and above them rises a two hundred foot bell tower of pink marble —reflected in the cool mirror of a lake at its base.

THE SPINSTER WHO TURNED DOWN THE MARRIAGE PROPOSALS OF A THOUSAND MEN AND RIDES A SNORTING, BUCKING HORSE

THE most wonderful woman I have ever known has had a thousand men propose to her. She has turned down offers from millionaires and from fishermen and farmers and penniless men on the Bowery. A prince from one of Europe's most prominent royal families followed her for months and begged her to marry him. And now, although she has already reached her three-score years and ten, she is still getting so many proposals by mail that her secretary doesn't even bother to show them to her.

Her name is Evangeline Booth, and she is the head of the grandest army that ever attacked an enemy—the Salvation Army—an army with thirty thousand officers, feeding the hungry in eighty-six far-flung countries and spreading love in eighty different languages.

I got something of a shock when I met Evangeline Booth. I knew she was old enough to be a grandmother, yet her dark red hair was just beginning to show a few streaks of gray. And she was sparkling with vivacity and blazing with enthusiasm.

Talk about life beginning at forty! If you ever saw this woman mount a horse that is so wild and jumpy

EVANGELINE BOOTH
The killer of the Klondike knelt down and prayed

that it takes two men to hold him, you would believe that life begins at seventy. Evangeline Booth bought the horse cheap because his owner was afraid to ride him. His name is Golden Heart, and when she mounts Golden Heart and shouts, "Let him go!" Golden Heart jumps and plunges and goes backwards and forwards and sideways all over the lot before she can quiet him down. She rides for an hour every morning—sometimes she holds the reins in one hand and a speech in the other and prepares a talk while she is galloping through the woods.

Every summer when she is in America, she goes to Lake George and does fancy diving—jack-knives and turtle-backs and swan-dives; and when she was sixty-three, she swam clear across Lake George in four hours.

She sleeps every night with a paper pad beside her bed, and often she awakes in the middle of the night and writes down a sheaf of notes. One night when she couldn't sleep, she got up at 3:00 A. M. and composed the words and music to a song. She has three secretaries living in the house with her; and she sometimes gets one out of bed at 2:00 A. M. and begins work.

It takes her an hour to motor from her house to the office; and she dictates all that time in her automobile.

Evangeline Booth says that one of the most thrilling experiences of her life occurred during the gold rush to the Yukon. You may recall that just before the turn of the Century, gold was discovered in Alaska, and the news set the nation seething with excitement. Hordes of men began hurrying to the far North, and Evangeline Booth knew that the Salvation Army would be needed there; so with a couple of trained nurses and three or four assistants, she headed for the Yukon. When she landed in Skagway, eggs were worth twenty-five cents apiece, and butter sold for three dollars a pound. Some men were hungry and all of them carried guns. And everywhere she heard men talking about "Soapy" Smith, the killer of the Klondike, the Dillinger of the Yukon. "Soapy" Smith and his gang laid in wait for miners returning from the gold fields and shot them down without warning and robbed them of their gold dust. The United States Government sent an armed posse to kill him; but "Soapy" Smith shot all of them and escaped.

Skagway was a tough place. Five men were killed there the day Evangeline Booth arrived.

That night, she held a meeting on the banks of the Yukon River; and preached to twenty-five thousand lonely men and got all of them singing songs they had heard their mothers sing in the long ago—*Jesus, Lover of My Soul, Nearer My God To Thee*, and *Home, Sweet, Home*.

The Arctic night was chilly and raw and cold, so while she was singing, one man brought a blanket and threw it around her.

This vast crowd of men sang until one o'clock in the morning; and then Evangeline Booth and her helpers went out in the forest to sleep on the ground under the pine trees. They had started a fire and were making a little cocoa when they saw five men approaching them with guns. When they got within speaking distance, the head man took off his hat and said, "I'm 'Soapy' Smith; and I've come to tell you how much I enjoyed your singing." And he added, "I was the man that sent you the blanket while you were singing. You can keep it, if you want to." A blanket doesn't sound like much of a gift now; but it was a royal present up there where men were dying from chills and the damp.

She asked him if she would be in any danger there in

Skagway. "No. Not while I'm here," he said. "I'll protect you."

She talked with him in the white night of the midnight Sun for three hours. She said, "I'm giving life and you're taking it. That's not right. You can't win. They'll kill you sooner or later." She talked to him of his childhood and his mother; and he told her that he used to attend Salvation Army meetings with his grandmother and sing and clap his hands. And he confessed that when his grandmother lay dying, she asked him to sing a song they had learned together at the Salvation Army meetings:

> *My heart is now whiter than snow,*
> *For Jesus abides with me here.*
> *My sins which are many, I know*
> *Are pardoned. My title is clear.*

Miss Booth asked him to kneel with her; and the Salvation Army girl and "Soapy" Smith, the most notorious bandit that ever terrorized the North, got down on their knees together and prayed and wept together under the northern pines. With tears rolling down his cheeks, "Soapy" promised her that he would stop killing people and would give himself up, and Miss Booth promised that she would use all her influence with the government to get him a light sentence.

At four o'clock in the morning, he left her.

At nine o'clock, he sent one of his men to her with a present of freshly baked bread and jam tartlets and a pound of butter—delicacies that were priceless up there. He had stuck people up with a gun and stolen the flour and the butter, and one of the bad women of Skagway had requested the privilege of baking the bread and jam tartlets for the good woman who had come to Alaska to preach love and purity and forgiveness.

Two days later, somebody shot "Soapy" Smith and Skagway erected a monument to the honor of the man who killed him.

Evangeline Booth is one of the happiest persons I have ever met. Happy because she is living for others. She told me that the deepest passion of her life is a desire to make every person she meets—even every waitress and pullman porter—a little better because she has passed that way.

THE MYSTERY MAN WHO MAY HAVE BEEN
RESPONSIBLE FOR THE DEATH OF
SOMEONE YOU KNOW

ZAHAROFF—that was the name of one of the richest, one of the most mysterious, and one of the most bitterly condemned men on earth. Twenty years ago, a reward of a hundred thousand dollars was offered to anyone who would kill him. Numerous books were written about him; he was one of the most amazing phenomena of international suspicion and national hate.

Born in the most terrible poverty, Basil Zaharoff lived to amass one of the greatest fortunes on earth. And he did it by selling machine guns and cannon and high explosives. One of his biographies began with these words: "The gravestones of a million men shall be his monument —their dying groans his epitaph."

When Zaharoff was twenty-eight years old, he got a job selling ammunition for $25. a week and commissions. He was living in Greece at the time; and he knew that the only way to sell guns was to create a demand for them. So he whipped up the fears of the Greeks, and told them they were surrounded by blood-thirsty enemies and must buy guns to defend their fatherland. That was more than half a century ago. A wave of excitement swept over the country. Bands played. Flags waved. Orators harangued the crowds; and Greece increased its

Redrawn from a sketch by S. T. Woolf. Reproduced by permission.

BASIL ZAHAROFF

A reward of $100,000. was offered to anyone who would
kill this man

army and bought guns from Zaharoff, and also a sub-
marine—one of the first war submarines ever built.

Having made several million dollars in commissions out
of that deal, Zaharoff ran over to the Turks and said,
"Look what the Greeks are doing. They are getting
ready to wipe you off the face of the earth." So the
Turks bought two submarines. The arms race was on,
and Zaharoff had launched himself on a career that was
destined to net him three hundred million dollars, all
drenched with blood.

For more than half a century Zaharoff fattened on national fears, arming traditional enemies and helping to
foment wars. During the Russian-Japanese conflict, he
sold ammunition to both sides. During the Spanish-
American War, he sold the bullets that killed American
soldiers. During the World War, he owned stock in
munition factories in Germany, England, France and
Italy; so his wealth mounted and skyrocketed at a rate
that staggers the imagination.

For half a century, he slipped in and out among the
war offices of Europe with the silence of a cat—cloaking
his movements in the utmost secrecy.

He was said to have employed two men who looked
precisely like him. Their sole duty was to appear in public so that the newspapers would report him in Berlin
or Monte Carlo when in reality he was on a secret mission to some other city. He never willingly posed for a
photograph. He never granted an interview, and he never
defended, never explained, never struck back, never answered the scathing denunciations that were heaped
upon him.

When he was twenty-six years old—handsome, tall,
and dashing—he fell romantically in love with a young
woman of seventeen. He met her on a train while travel-

ing from Athens to Paris, and wanted to marry her at once; but she, unfortunately, was already wedded to a Spanish Duke who was half-mad and twice her age. Divorce was impossible because of her religious beliefs. So Zaharoff waited for her—waited and cherished her in his heart for almost half a century. Finally, in 1923, her husband died in an insane asylum; and in 1924, she married Zaharoff. She was sixty-five at the time, and he was seventy-four years old. Two years later she died. She had been his sweetheart for forty-eight years, and his wife for eighteen months.

Until his death, he spent his summers in a magnificent chateau near Paris; but he was born in far-off Turkey in a mud hut that had no windows. As a child, he slept on a dirt floor, tied rags around his feet to keep them warm, and often went hungry.

He attended school for only five years, but he spoke fourteen languages, and Oxford University honored him with the title of Doctor of Civil Law.

The first time he appeared in London, he was jailed as a thief. Thirty years later, he was knighted by the King of England.

One day in the summer of 1909, this mystery man of Europe was walking through the famous Zoological Gardens in Paris; and he was shocked to see that the monkeys in the Zoo were mangy and hungry, and that the most famous lion in the Zoo was suffering from rheumatism. Everything about the place seemed to be going to rack and ruin. So Zaharoff called for the manager and scolded him sharply. The manager didn't realize he was talking to one of the wealthiest men in the world, so he replied rather tartly that he didn't have the half million francs necessary to take care of the animals properly. Zaharoff said. "Well, if that's all you need, here it is," and this man whose bullets had killed a million men, wrote out a check for a hundred thousand dollars to care for some animals. The manager, unable to decipher the signature, thought the stranger was trying to play a trick on him; so he tossed the check on to a pile of other papers and forgot all about it. Months later, he showed it to a friend and was astonished to learn that it was real, that it was signed by the wealthiest man in France.

Zaharoff died at eighty-five, a lonely, tragic figure, broken in health. A servant pushed him about in a wheel chair, and his chief interest in life seemed to be his garden of lovely roses. He had been writing his diary for half a century; it filled fifty-three books; and rumor has it that he ordered all those secret records to be destroyed at his death.

BILLY SUNDAY

Sometimes he stood with one foot on the pulpit

THE BALLPLAYER WHO LED A MILLION
SOULS DOWN THE SAWDUST TRAIL
TO SALVATION

THE most popular preacher in the history of the Christian pulpit was an ex-boozefighter and ex-ballplayer—Billy Sunday.

Eighty million people—two thirds of all the men, women and children in America—flocked to hear his rough-and-ready, rip-snorting message of sin and salvation.

It was his favorite boast that during his thirty-five years of lambasting the devil, he had led more than a million souls down the sawdust trail toward the Light, and he was probably the greatest single power in bringing about Prohibition.

I saw Billy Sunday many times. He was a fury, a human dynamo in trousers. I saw him thump his chest, tear off his coat, collar and tie, leap up on chairs, stand with one foot on the pulpit, and then fling himself on the floor in imitation of a ballplayer sliding into home plate. Nobody ever went to sleep listening to Billy Sunday. His sermons were as entertaining as a circus. He preached so strenuously that he carried a physical trainer with him and never a day passed that he didn't get a pummeling and a rub-down.

He preached in Pittsburgh for eight weeks and the

newspapers reported his meetings with flaring headlines every day. The whole town was excited. Big department stores sent their employees en masse to hear him. Factory girls attended the noon-day meetings in crowds. One day, ten policemen stepped forward before an audience of fifteen thousand people and declared themselves on the side of the Lord.

Unlike most evangelists, Billy Sunday appealed mostly to men. He used to say: "I am a rube of the rubes. The odor of the barnyard is on me yet. I have greased my hair with goose grease and blacked my boots with stove blacking. I have wiped my old proboscis with a gunny-sack towel, I have drunk coffee out of my saucer, and I have eaten with my knife. I have said 'done it' when I should have said 'did it,' and I have said 'I have saw' when I should have said 'I have seen,' and I expect to go to heaven just the same."

He was born in a log cabin in Iowa and reared in an orphan asylum. When he was fifteen, he got a job as janitor in a school. This job paid him $25. a month and gave him a chance to get an education. All he had to do was to get up at two o'clock in the morning, carry coal for fourteen stoves, keep all fourteen fires going during the day, sweep and polish the floors, and then keep abreast in his studies.

His first real job was as assistant to an undertaker in Marshalltown, Iowa. It was while holding down that job that he began to make a name for himself as a ballplayer.

He could run the bases so fast that Pop Anson, leader of the Chicago White Sox, sent for him; and before Billy Sunday was twenty-one, he was a star performer in the big leagues. "I could circle those bases in fourteen seconds," he used to say, "and that's a record that's never been beaten."

It was five years after he left the undertaker's shop that the revelation occurred which changed him from a hard-drinking ballplayer into the most hypnotic preacher since the days of John Wesley.

Here is what happened to him—and now I am quoting Billy Sunday's own words:

"One day in 1887, I was walking down a street in Chicago in company with some famous ballplayers. We went into a saloon. It was Sunday afternoon and we got tanked up and then went and sat down on a corner. Across the street a company of men and women were playing on instruments—horns, flutes and slide trombones—and the others were singing the gospel hymns that I used to hear my mother sing back in the log cabin in Iowa, and I sobbed and sobbed. Then a young man stepped out and said, 'We are going down to the Pacific Garden Mission. Won't you come down to the Mission with us? I am sure you will enjoy it. You will hear drunkards tell how they have been saved and girls tell how they have been saved from the red-light district.'

"I arose and said to the boys, 'I'm through. I am going to Jesus Christ. We've come to the parting of the ways,' and I turned my back on them. Some of them laughed and some of them mocked me; but one of them gave me encouragement."

That is the way he described his own conversion.

The skeptics and scoffers used to accuse Billy Sunday of exploiting religious hunger for the mere sake of money. Yet the truth is, he gave up a salary of five hundred dollars a month as a ball player to work for the Y.M.C.A. for eighty-three dollars a month—and it was sometimes six months before he collected even that!

I remember Billy Sunday when he came to New York in 1917. Never before or since has the town called

Babylon-on-the-Hudson seen such a frenzy of religious excitement. His arrival was heralded months in advance. At least twenty thousand prayer meetings were held in preparation for his coming. Up at 168th Street and Broadway, four hundred workers labored furiously to complete a tabernacle capable of seating twenty thousand, and four carloads of sawdust were sprinkled on the floor to make the famous sawdust trail. Two thousand chairs were placed upon the platform for the choir alone; and two thousand ushers, working in shifts of seven hundred each, volunteered for the honor of showing the faithful to their seats.

During his stay in New York, Billy Sunday preached to a million and a quarter people; and nearly a hundred thousand sinners came forward and renounced their evil ways.

HE WAS SHOT IN THE BREAST; BUT HE
KEPT RIGHT ON WITH HIS SPEECH

A N INCIDENT happened in January 1919 that I shall never forget. I was in the army at the time—stationed at Camp Upton on Long Island. One afternoon a detachment of soldiers marched up a hill, raised their rifles into the air, and fired a salute. Roosevelt was dead! Theodore Roosevelt, the most colorful and spectacular president that ever wielded a big stick over this nation! He died a comparatively young man. If he were still living, he would be just one year younger than Clarence Darrow—only four years older than Hearst.

Almost everything about Teddy Roosevelt was extraordinary. For example, even though he was so nearsighted that, without his glasses, he couldn't recognize his best friend ten feet away, he became an expert rifle shot and brought down charging lions in Africa.

He was the most famous big-game hunter of all time; yet he never went fishing, and never shot a bird.

As a boy, he was pale and sickly and tortured with asthma; so he went west for his health, became a cowboy, slept out under the stars, and developed such a magnificent physique that he boxed with Mike Donovan. He explored the wilderness of South America, climbed such mountains as the Jungfrau and the Matterhorn, and led a mighty charge up San Juan Hill in Cuba in the face of deadly rifle fire.

THEODORE ROOSEVELT

He slept with a loaded revolver beside his pillow in the
White House

Roosevelt says in his autobiography that as a child he was nervous and timid and afraid of getting hurt; yet he broke his wrist, his arm, his nose, his ribs, and his shoulder, and kept right on taking chances. When he was a cowboy in Dakota, he'd be thrown from his horse, crack a bone, climb into the saddle again, and go on rounding up cattle.

He says that he developed courage by doing the things he was afraid to do—by acting as if he were brave even though he were half scared to death. He finally became so courageous he didn't fear even roaring lions or blazing cannon.

During the Bull Moose campaign in 1912, a half-crazy man shot Roosevelt in the breast while he was on his way to make a speech. Roosevelt didn't let anybody know that the bullet had struck him. He went right on to the auditorium and started to speak and kept on speaking until he almost collapsed from loss of blood. Then he was rushed to the hospital.

When he was in the White House, he slept with a loaded revolver by his pillow, and he carried a small pistol whenever he went out for a walk.

While he was President, he was boxing with an army officer. The soldier hit him squarely in the left eye, broke the blood vessels, and permanently injured his sight. Roosevelt didn't want the young man to realize what he had done; so when the officer asked him to box again, the President said no, he guessed he was getting too old to box. Years later, he lost the sight of that eye completely, but he never let the captain of artillery know what had happened.

He chopped all the firewood used on his estate at Oyster Bay, pitched hay in the field with the farm hands, and insisted on his gardener's paying him the same wages he paid the rest of the help.

He never smoked, he never swore, and about the only drinking he ever did was to take a teaspoo· ⸀ul of brandy, on rare occasions, in a milk-shake at night. He didn't even know there was any brandy in the milk-shake until his valet told him about it; yet he was called a hard drinker so often that he finally had to bring a libel suit to stop the slander.

Busy as he was, he found time to read hundreds and hundreds of books while he was in the White House. He would often have the entire forenoon packed tight with a series of five-minute interviews; but he kept a book by his side to utilize even the few spare seconds that elapsed between his callers.

When he went traveling, he usually carried a pocket edition of Shakespeare or Bobbie Burns. Once when he was punching cattle in Dakota, he sat beside a flickering campfire and read the whole of *Hamlet* aloud to a cowboy. On his trip through the jungles of Brazil, he spent his evenings reading Gibbons' *Decline and Fall of the Roman Empire*.

He loved music, but he couldn't carry a tune himself. While he was working alone, he often tried to sing *Nearer My God To Thee*. Once he rode through the streets of a western town, tipping his hat to the cheering throngs, and all the while, he kept singing to himself *Nearer My God To Thee*.

He had many hobbies. Once, when he was in the White House, he telephoned a well-known Washington newspaper correspondent to come to the Executive Mansion at once. This newspaper reporter, excited by the request, imagined he was going to have an exclusive interview about some affair of state; so he wired his paper to hold the presses ready to dash off an extra immediately.

When the reporter arrived at the White House, Roosevelt didn't say a word about politics, instead, he led the reporter out to an old hollow tree in the White House yard and showed him a nest of young owls he had discovered.

On a train trip through the West at one time, he was talking to a group of executives in his private car. Suddenly he saw a farmer standing in his corn field beside the tracks, with his hat off. Roosevelt knew the man was paying his respects to the President of the United States; so he jumped up, rushed to the rear platform, and waved his hat furiously. He didn't do that as a political stunt. He did it because deep in his heart, he liked people.

During the last year of his life, his health began to fail, and, although he was only sixty, he remarked several times that he was getting old. He wrote a letter to an aged friend saying: "You and I are within reach of the rifle pits, and any moment we may go down into the darkness."

He died peacefully in his sleep, on January 4, 1919. The last words he ever uttered were: "Please put out the lights."

WOODROW WILSON
He longed for friends—and made millions of enemies

HE WAS FACED WITH ONE OF THE GREATEST OPPORTUNITIES IN HISTORY; YET HE FAILED BECAUSE HE COULDN'T HANDLE PEOPLE

WHAT kind of man was the real Woodrow Wilson?

He has been called a supreme genius; he has also been called a magnificent failure.

He saw a vision of world peace—the League of Nations—and on the altar of that vision, he consecrated every ounce of his vitality and his strength—finally he died, a man shattered by his own ideal.

When Woodrow Wilson sailed for Europe in 1919, he was called the savior of the ages. Bleeding Europe hailed him as a god. Starving peasants burned candles before his picture and offered up prayers to him as though he were a saint.

The whole world lay at his feet. Yet when he returned to this country three months later, a sick and broken man, he had alienated many friends and made a hundred million enemies.

History presents Woodrow Wilson as an idealistic school-teacher—cold, dignified, and lacking in human warmth. Yet the truth is almost exactly the opposite. Wilson was intensely human—hungry for human relationships—and it was the sorrow of his life that his own shyness kept him aloof and apart.

"I would give anything in the world if I were different," he said, "but I cannot make myself over."

Sometimes he could unbend. When he was a professor at Wesleyan University, he jumped down out of the bleachers one day and led the cheering at a football game. And when he was in Bermuda, he went sailing for the sheer pleasure of chatting with the negro boatmen.

Woodrow Wilson was probably the most scholarly man who ever sat in the White House, yet he couldn't read or write until he was eleven years old. His favorite reading for relaxation was detective stories.

He cared little for art. He often said that he would rather have a chromo that you can buy in a ten cent store than a Whistler etching.

And this highbrow professor who had spent his life in the cloistered atmosphere of academies frankly said that he would rather see a musical comedy than a Shakespearian play. He said he didn't go to the theatre to be edified. He went there to be entertained—and when he was in the White House, he went to vaudeville shows almost every week.

Most of his life he had been poor. His salary as a teacher was so small that his wife painted pictures and sold them to help support the family.

As a young professor, Woodrow Wilson couldn't afford to buy good clothes; and later in life, like Lincoln, he cared little about his personal appearance. For example, when he was President, his valet urged him to send his old dress-suit to the tailor to have the lapels refaced with new satin; but Woodrow Wilson said, "No, don't bother. That is good for a year yet."

And like Lincoln, Wilson was indifferent to food. He

ate whatever was set before him and often seemed to be unconscious of what he was eating.

He smoked only one cigar in his life—or rather, he didn't smoke all of even one, for he got sick before he finished it.

His only extravagance was buying beautiful books.

Under his frozen exterior, Woodrow Wilson was a man of quick and fierce emotion. Those who knew him said he had a hotter temper than Theodore Roosevelt. His devotion to his first wife was intense and pathetic. One of his first acts after he became President was to buy his wife a set of sable furs. When she died a year later, he would not permit her body to be removed from the White House for seventy-two hours. He had it laid on a sofa, and for three days and three nights, he would not leave her side.

He was regarded as an intellectual giant; but he had little command of languages, he was unacquainted with much of the world's great literature, he was indifferent to science, and he cared very little for philosophy.

He started out in life to be a lawyer, but at law he was a dismal failure. He never conducted a case by himself in his life, and he handled property for only one client— his mother.

Probably the greatest flaw in Wilson's character was his lack of tact. The ambition of his whole life, from his boyhood on, was to become a statesman. He practiced public speaking in his room for hours at a time. In order to perfect himself, he did futile things, for example, he even posted a chart on his wall showing how to make appropriate gestures. But he overlooked the most important thing of all—he never learned how to handle people. The last years of his life were a tragic series of broken friendships. He quarreled with the leaders of the Senate.

He broke off with his closest friends such as Colonel House. Finally, he alienated many of the people of his own country by asking them to elect only Democrats to office.

When the Senate refused to accept the League of Nations, Wilson appealed directly to the people. His health had always been delicate and his physicians warned him against any additional strain. But he ignored their advice.

During the last year of the Presidency, this intellectual genius whose words had once shaken the world, was now so broken and weak that he couldn't sign his own name without someone guiding his hand.

After his retirement, people came from all over the world to his house on S Street in Washington—came to it as though it were a shrine. And when he lay dying, pilgrims knelt on the pavement before his house and prayed for the passing of his soul.

THE "TOUGH GUY" WHO WENT THROUGH HIGH-SCHOOL IN THREE MONTHS AND WROTE FIFTY-ONE BOOKS IN EIGHTEEN YEARS

A LITTLE over forty years ago, a hobo rode the rods of a freight train into Buffalo and began to beg for food from door to door. A policeman arrested him for vagrancy, and a judge sentenced him to thirty days at hard labor in the penitentiary. For thirty days, he broke rocks and had nothing whatever to eat except bread and water.

Yet six years later—only six years later, mind you, this hobo, this former bum and panhandler, was the most sought-after man on the Western coast. He was entertained by the cream of California society and hailed by novelists, critics, and editors, as one of the brightest stars on the literary horizon.

He never went to high school until he was nineteen, and he died when he was forty; but he left behind him fifty-one books.

He was Jack London, author of *The Call of the Wild*. When Jack London wrote *The Call of the Wild* back in 1903, he became famous overnight. Editors clamored for his work. But he made very little money from his first big hit. The publishers—and later the movie producers in Hollywood—made a million dollars out of it;

JACK LONDON

The judge said: "Thirty days!"—and six years later
society was begging for his autograph

but he himself sold all his rights to *The Call of the Wild* for only two thousand dollars.

If you want to write a book, the very first requisite is to have something to write about. That was one of the secrets of Jack London's astonishing success. He packed ten thousand colorful experiences into his short and feverish life. He was a sailor before the mast, a longshoreman, an oyster-pirate, and a gold miner. He hunted seals in the far North. He hoboed over half the earth, and wrote a book about his experiences as a tramp. He often went hungry. He slept on park benches and in hay stacks and box cars. He often slept on the hard ground—and sometimes woke up and found himself sleeping in a pool of water. He was so exhausted at times that he fell asleep while riding the rods underneath a freight train.

He was arrested and thrown into jails hundreds of times here in America and he was clamped into the jails of Mexico, Manchuria, Japan and Korea.

Jack London's childhood was seared with poverty and hardships. He ran wild with a gang of hoodlums who roamed the water-front along San Francisco Bay. School? He laughed at schools and played hookey most of the time. Yet one day he wandered into a public library and began reading *Robinson Crusoe*. He was fascinated. Hungry as he was, he didn't even stop to run home for supper. The next day, he rushed back to the library to read other books. A new world was opening up before him—a world as strange and colorful as the Bagdad of the *Arabian Nights*. From that time on, he had an unquenchable passion for books. He often read ten and fifteen hours a day. He devoured everything from Nick Carter to Shakespeare—everything from Herbert Spencer to Karl Marx. When he was nineteen, he decided to stop selling his muscles and sell his brain instead. He was tired of hoboing, tired of being beaten up by police-men, tired of having railroad brakemen hit him over the head with their lanterns.

So, at the age of nineteen, he entered high school in Oakland, California. He studied night and day, took hardly any time at all for sleep and did a phenomenal thing. He actually crammed four years of work into three months, passed his examinations, and then entered the University of California.

Obsessed with a driving ambition to become a great writer, he studied *Treasure Island*, *The Count of Monte Cristo*, and *The Tale of Two Cities*—studied them over and over and then wrote feverishly. He wrote five thou-sand words a day, that means a full length novel in twenty days. He sometimes had thirty stories out in the hands of editors at the same time. But they all came back. He was merely learning his trade.

Then one day one of his stories entitled *Typhoon Off the Coast of Japan* won first prize in a contest sponsored by the *San Francisco Call*. He got only twenty dollars for the story. He was broke, and couldn't pay even his room rent.

That was 1896—a year of drama and excitement. Gold was discovered in the Klondike. Telegraph wires flashed the sensational news across the continent and thrilled the nation. Workmen left their shops, soldiers deserted from the army, farmers abandoned their lands, merchants locked their stores. The gold-diggers were on the move. The locust swarm of humanity took wings and headed for the golden land under the northern lights.

And Jack London was with them. He spent a hectic year hunting for gold in the Klondike. He endured in-credible hardships. Eggs were worth twenty-five cents apiece and butter sold for three dollars a pound. He slept on the ground with the thermometer at 74 degrees below zero. Finally he drifted back to the States without a penny in his pocket.

He did whatever odd jobs he could find. He washed dishes in restaurants. He scrubbed floors. He worked on the docks and in factories.

Then one day, with only two dollars between himself and hunger, he decided to give up manual labor forever and devote all of his time to literature. That was in 1898. Five years later, in 1903, he had published six books and one hundred and twenty-five short stories, and was one of the most talked-of men in literary America.

Jack London died in 1916, only eighteen years after he really started to write, and during that time, he wrote an average of about three books a year besides countless stories.

And his yearly income was twice as much as the President of the United States. His books are still enormously popular and in Europe, he is one of the most widely read of all American authors.

The Call of the Wild, for which he got only two thousand dollars, has been translated into a score of languages. It has sold more than a million and a half copies and is one of the most popular books in the history of American literature.

Redrawn from a sketch by G. Maillard Kesslere. Courtesy of the artist.

HELEN JEPSON

They called her "Fatty," and she sold corsets in a department store

A DARN IN HER STOCKING SET HER FEET
ON THE LADDER TO FAME

DO YOU like Cinderella stories? Well, here is one that actually happened.

This is the story of a little girl who was once called "Fatty," but who grew up to be one of the most beautiful singers of all time.

This is the story of a little girl who was so poor she couldn't afford to take music lessons; yet she is now a prima donna in the Metropolitan Opera Company in New York.

In 1930, this girl had one radio audition after another, and nobody wanted her. Four years later, the radio editors of America voted her the most important new radio personality of the year.

One season while I was broadcasting over the Columbia network, I often admired a beautiful platinum blonde sitting in the front row of the studio audience—a glamorous blonde with soft brown eyes, a stunning figure, and personal charm. Finally I met her—and discovered she was none other than the famous Helen Jepson, and that she was the wife of George Possell, the flute player in the orchestra.

I asked George if it was a case of love at first sight, and he said, "Yes," but Helen Jepson broke in to say, "Yes, it was love at first sight on *my* part, but not on his.

153

I loved him for years," she said, "before he would pay any attention to me. I used to even walk around the block where he lived—walk around it time after time hoping I could meet him—and then one day I caught a glimpse of him behind a screen door and was so frightened that I ran. I first saw him when he was playing in the orchestra at Chautauqua Lake. I was only twenty at the time," she said, "and he was thirty-two. I was nobody, and he was at the top of his profession. And I was so deeply in love with him that I used to hide behind trees to watch him pass."

I asked Helen Jepson what was the most astonishing thing she knew about herself and she said: "Well, most people are surprised to know I am married and have a baby."

I asked the baby what her name was, and she said: "I am almost three."

I said: "Yes, but what's your name?" And she replied, "I am almost three."

"Yes, I know, but what's your name?" Again she replied, "I'm going to have ice cream and cake on my birthday."

She stuck right to fundamentals all the time.

I asked Helen Jepson if she is superstitious, to which she answered, "Oh no, I whistle in my dressing room at the Metropolitan and, you know, that is supposed to be the worst thing a singer can do."

When her baby was born, the nurse in the hospital put an identification tag around the baby's neck—a string of beads with the baby's name on it. Miss Jepson has had that tiny string of beads made into a little bracelet and she wouldn't dream of singing without wearing that bracelet or holding it in her hands.

I asked her if she didn't think that was superstitious,

"Oh, no. That's my good luck charm," was her retort.

If Helen Jepson hadn't sung *Carry Me Back to Old Virginia* before the Rotary Club in Akron, Ohio, she might still be selling corsets today instead of being one of the most talked-of figures in the musical world. It happened thus: She had always longed to be a singer. She had an aunt who was on the vaudeville stage and who used to send her some of the old costumes she had discarded. Little Helen used to dress up in these costumes and sing and dance and "play theatre" with the other children in the neighborhood. Later, in high school, she was a star performer in the glee club; after she graduated, she got a job selling corsets in a department store in Akron, Ohio. A dull job; but it enabled her to save nickels and dimes and go to Cleveland occasionally to take music lessons. She sang in the choir on Sundays, and sometimes dressed herself up in colonial costumes and sang before clubs and social organizations.

One day a business man heard her sing at the Rotary Club, heard her sing *Carry Me Back to Old Virginia.* He needed a sales girl to sell phonograph records in his store; so he gave her the job and changed the whole course of her life. In the music store, she played operatic records over and over again and tried to imitate them, and she sang with Jeritza and Bori and Rosa Ponselle. "Why," she said to me, "I have to pinch myself sometimes now to realize that it is really true that I know these famous singers whom I used to listen to in awe as they sang on the phonograph."

Finally, she had an opportunity to compete for a scholarship in the famous Curtis Institute of Music in Philadelphia. Should she go? It would take almost all her savings to buy a ticket to Philadelphia. She was only one of two hundred girls competing for the prize.

Suppose she failed? Well, if she failed, she wouldn't have enough money to get back home. She would have to get a job selling corsets in Philadelphia. But if she succeeded—if she succeeded, she would be standing on the threshold of fairyland. So she gambled on her future and went to Philadelphia. Some of the other two hundred contestants had voices just as sweet and clear and colorful as hers. But she had something they didn't have. She had showmanship, the ability to sell herself, the ability to put her songs across. And then one of the judges noticed that Helen had a neat little darn in one of her stockings; and this judge liked girls who had sense enough to darn their stockings. So Helen Jepson won the scholarship.

She and another girl rented a room on the outskirts of the city. They had to walk up five flights; and on cold winter days, they sat on one another's feet and rocked back and forth to keep warm. They lighted candles and put them on the floor and imagined they had a fireplace. They had only fifty cents a day to spend on food, so they cooked their meals over a little gas burner. Sometimes they had nothing but soup for dinner; but they sang songs from *La Bôheme* and imagined that they were in Paris. Hardships? Not a bit of it. They were having the time of their lives.

One of the things I admire most about Helen Jepson is the fact that success and fame and money haven't spoiled her. She is just as democratic and unassuming now as she was fifteen years ago when she was sweeping the floor and frying pork chops for her father back in Akron, Ohio.

HE MADE MORE MILLIONAIRES THAN
ANY MAN WHO EVER LIVED

ANDREW CARNEGIE was born without benefit of doctor or midwife because his people were too poor to afford either. He started working for two cents an hour—and he made four hundred million dollars.

Once I visited the cottage in Dunfermline, Scotland, where he was born. The house had only two rooms. His father ran a weaving business on the ground floor and the family cooked and ate and slept in one tiny, dark attic room upstairs.

When the Carnegie family came to America, Andrew's father made tablecloths and peddled them from door to door. His mother took in washing and stitched boots for a shoemaker. Andrew had only one shirt, so his mother washed and ironed that shirt every night after he had gone to bed. She worked for sixteen to eighteen hours a day, and Andrew adored her. When he was twenty-two, he promised her that he would never marry as long as she lived. And he didn't. He didn't marry until his mother died thirty years later. He was fifty-two when he married and sixty-two when his first and only child was born.

As a boy, he said to his mother over and over: "Mother, I am going to be rich some day so that you can have silk dresses and servants and a carriage of your

157

ANDREW CARNEGIE
One day an inventor came along and sat down beside him

own." He often said that he inherited all his brains from his mother, that his undying love for her was one of the driving forces of his spectacular career. When she died, his grief was so intense that he couldn't bear to speak her name for fifteen years. He once paid the mortgage on an old woman's house in Scotland merely because she looked like his mother.

Andrew Carnegie was known as the steel king; yet he knew very little about the manufacture of steel. He had hundreds, perhaps thousands, of men working for him who knew more about steel than he did. But he knew how to handle men—and that is what made him rich. Early in life, he showed a flare for organization, for leadership, for making other people work for him.

When he was a boy in Scotland, he got hold of a mother rabbit. Presto! He soon had a whole nest of little rabbits—and nothing to feed them. But he had a brilliant idea. He told the boys in the neighborhood that if they would go out and pull enough clover and dandelions to feed the rabbits, he would name the bunnies in their honor. The plan worked like magic.

Years later, Carnegie used the same psychology in business. For example, he wanted to sell steel rails to the Pennsylvania Railroad. Mr. J. Edgar Thomson was the president of the Pennsylvania Railroad at that time. So Andrew Carnegie built a huge steel mill in Pittsburgh and called it the "J. Edgar Thomson Steel Works." Naturally, Mr. Thomson was delighted, and it didn't take much persuasion to get him to order his steel rails from the company that bore his name.

Carnegie got a job as a telegraph messenger boy in Pittsburgh. The pay was fifty cents a day. It seemed like a fortune. He was a stranger in town. He was afraid he might lose his position, because he didn't know how to get about, so he memorized the names and addresses of every firm in the business section of the city. He longed to be an operator; so he studied telegraphy at night and rushed down to the office early each morning to practise on the keys.

One morning the wire was hot with big news. Philadelphia was calling Pittsburgh, calling frantically. There was no operator on duty. So Andrew Carnegie rushed to the wire, took the message, delivered it, and was immediately promoted to the position of operator with his salary doubled.

His restless energy, his sleepless ambition attracted attention. The Pennsylvania railroad erected a telegraph line of its own. Andrew Carnegie was made operator, then private secretary to the division superintendent.

Suddenly one day an event happened that started him on the way to fortune. An inventor came and sat down beside him in a railroad train and showed him the model of a new sleeping car he had invented. The sleeping cars of that day were crude bunks nailed to the sides of freight cars. This new invention was much like the Pullman car of today. Carnegie had shrewd Scotch foresight. He saw that the invention had possibilities—enormous possibilities. So he borrowed money and bought stock in the concern. The company paid sensational dividends and when Andrew Carnegie reached twenty-five, his annual income from this one investment alone was five thousand dollars a year.

Once a wooden bridge burned on the railroad and tied up traffic for days. Andrew Carnegie was a division superintendent at the time. Wooden bridges were doomed. He saw that. Iron was the coming thing. So he borrowed money, formed a company, started building iron bridges—and the profits poured in so fast that he was almost dizzy.

This son of a weaver had the golden touch. He rode high, wide and handsome. Luck was with him, phenomenal luck. He and some friends bought a farm amidst the oil fields of Western Pennsylvania for forty thousand dollars and made a million dollars out of it in one year. By the time this canny Scot had reached twenty-seven, he had an income of a thousand dollars a week—and fifteen years before he had been working for twenty cents a day.

It was 1862 now. Abe Lincoln was in the White House. The Civil War was raging. Prices were skyrocketing. Big things were happening. Frontiers were being pushed back. The far West was opening up. Railroads were soon to be thrown across the continent. Cities were to be built. America trembled on the threshold of an astonishing era.

And Andy Carnegie, with the smoke and flames belching from his steel furnaces, rode up on a tidal wave of prosperity—rode and kept on riding until he had acquired riches such as had never been dreamed of before in the history of mankind.

Yet he never worked very hard. He played about half of the time. He said that he surrounded himself with assistants who knew more than he did—and he spurred them on to pile up millions for him. He was Scotch, but he wasn't too Scotch. He let his partners share in his profits and he made more millionaires than any other man who has ever lived.

He went to school only four years in his life; but in spite of that he wrote eight books of travel, biography, essays and economics and gave away sixty million dollars to public libraries, and seventy-eight millions for the advancement of education.

He memorized all the poems that Bobbie Burns ever wrote; and he could repeat from memory all of *Macbeth*, all of *Hamlet*, all of *King Lear, Romeo and Juliet*, and all of *The Merchant of Venice*.

He was not a member of any church, but he gave away more than seven thousand pipe organs to churches.

He gave away three hundred and sixty-five million dollars. That means he gave away a million dollars for every day in the year. Newspapers ran contests and offered prizes to those who could best tell him how to give away his hoard of gold. For he declared it was a disgrace to die rich.

HE ONCE PICKED GRAPES TO PAY HIS
RENT—TODAY HE EARNS FIVE
DOLLARS A SECOND

IN 1922, Lawrence Tibbett was living near Los Angeles having a hard time trying to support his wife. He sang in a church choir on Sunday, and picked up five dollars now and then by singing *Oh, Promise Me!* at a wedding.

He had studied for years; but he wasn't getting anywhere. However, he had a friend, Rupert Hughes, who believed in him. Hughes said: "You have the makings of a great voice. You ought to study in New York."

That little bit of friendly encouragement proved to be the turning point in Tibbett's life, for it caused him to borrow twenty-five hundred dollars and start East. What if he failed to make good in New York? Well, if he did, he was determined to go back to California and make a living selling automobile trucks.

That was in 1922. Is Lawrence Tibbett selling automobile trucks today? Far from it! He is now selling his services for thousands of dollars a week in Hollywood. You probably heard him sing in such motion pictures as *The Rogue Song, New Moon* and *The Cuban Love Song.*

And the next time you hear his stirring voice on the radio, it may interest you to recall that someone is paying

Redrawn from a sketch by Clarence Mattis. Permission of the artist.

LAWRENCE TIBBETT

They said he wasn't good enough to sing in their high
school glee-club

him three hundred dollars a minute, or five dollars a second, to sing to you.

In 1922, Lawrence Tibbett was so poor he couldn't afford to live in town. . . . So he rented a house in the country. Fortunately, the house stood in the middle of a vineyard; he got all the grapes he wanted to eat free; and he confessed that there were times when he had very little to eat except grapes. The house cost him only twelve dollars and fifty cents a month; but little as that was, it was sometimes more than he could make as a singer. He once got ten months behind in his rent and had to pick grapes and prune vines to pay off his debt.

He rented a piano for five dollars a month, but he couldn't put it in the front room because the rickety old house stood on a steep hillside and the front part of it was propped up on high stilts and he was afraid the piano would fall through the floor and go rolling and bouncing through the grape vines until it struck the bottom of the hill.

When he first came to New York, he couldn't afford to buy even the cheapest seat in the Metropolitan Opera House. So he used to pay two dollars and twenty cents for the privilege of standing up in the back of the mighty Metropolitan Opera House to listen to the glamorous performances of the immortal Scotti and the beautiful Mary Garden. In those days, he had to borrow money from his friends to pay for his room rent and music lessons.

Yet ten years later, he himself was striding across the proud stage of the Metropolitan, arousing a frenzy of wild huzzas, winning twenty-two curtain calls at a single performance and making himself one of the most famous baritones in all the world.

Every year there are hundreds of ambitious youngsters

with good voices who flock to New York, eager to win fame and fortune. I have often wondered how many of them fail to rise above mediocrity. I asked Lawrence Tibbett, and he said about nine hundred and ninety-nine out of every thousand; he added that the majority of them didn't fail because they lacked good voices, but because they lacked vocal intelligence. They failed, he said, because they had no gift for showmanship, no ability to grip their audience, to put their songs over, and make people feel what they were singing.

Lawrence Tibbett spent his childhood in Bekersfield, California. For years, his father had been a cowboy in California, riding the range, repairing fences, branding calves and battling with cattle rustlers. The old man carried a big pearl-handled revolver in his belt; he was a dead shot. He had two notches in his gun, because he had already killed two cattle thieves, and now he was sheriff of Kern County, California. He had a regular arsenal of guns in the house, and kept a huge bloodhound, with long ears and sad eyes, chained up in the back yard. Whenever a shooting occurred, the phone would ring and Sheriff Tibbett would grab his dog and gun, dash away to the scene of the crime, and put the bloodhound on the trail, and Rod—that was the old bloodhound's name—Rod would go bellowing across fields and through orchards and Sheriff Tibbett would run behind, holding on to the leash, waving his arms and crying: "Rod's got him this time. Rod's got him." But, instead of catching the criminal, Rod usually tracked down an old cow or a coyote.

Being a sheriff seemed like a mighty exciting and glamorous business to young Larry Tibbett, so his boyhood ambition was to be a sheriff himself like his father.

Then suddenly a dramatic and tragic thing happened.

His father was shot and killed in a battle with Jim Mc-Kinney, one of the most notorious bank robbers and gun men of the West.

That shooting changed the whole course of Lawrence Tibbett's life, for his father was a very religious man, bitterly opposed to smoking and dancing and card playing and the theatre; and Tibbett told me that if his father had not been shot, he himself would never have dared to become a singer and an actor. His father's training still casts a spell over him and even now he seldom smokes more than one cigar a year; and when he does, he has the feeling that he is doing something terribly wrong and that the devil is standing right by his side, urging him on to destruction.

As a boy in high school, Tibbett developed an inferiority complex. His mother ran a rooming house. He had only one suit of clothes, his trousers were too short, and he couldn't buy his best girl an ice cream soda at the corner drug store. The other students snubbed him and paid no attention to him. So he resolved to make a name for himself, and he looked about for a short cut to distinction. He tried to become a member of the glee club —and they wouldn't have him. He tried to get a part in the high school plays . . . and no one wanted him. This boy who was destined to become the most famous singer that ever came out of California was turned down cold when he wanted to sing in a high school concert. The spark of genius didn't shine through his voice until he was twenty-one years old.

Tibbett says that the greatest music is that which thrills you most and that a lot of our popular music is good, very good.

The End of a Perfect Day is the most popular song ever written. Five million people bought copies of it, and Lawrence Tibbett says that that humble song is a truly great one.

He believes that *Old Man River* and *The Rhapsody in Blue* are as fine as anything ever written by the greatest Viennese composers that ever lived.

ONE of the greatest movie stars in Hollywood today
is a genial gentleman with a big, red nose, a bay
window, and practically no hair on the top of his head.
In fact he's a little short on pulchritude—but Paramount
studios wouldn't swap him for the Apollo Belvedere.

This portly gentleman's name is Claude William
Dukenfield, and only two or three years ago he was
wearing out the seat of his pants sitting in casting rooms
and waiting to see directors. He had been a star for ten
years in the Ziegfeld Follies, and he had been in and out
of movies for the past twenty years. But he was so broke
that he offered to write, act, and direct a picture for
absolutely nothing, if only some producer would give
him a chance to come back. He thundered, begged, and
wheedled. But the answer was always the same: *No.
Absolutely no!*

But when *David Copperfield* finished production,
Claude William Dukenfield cashed a check for the rather
imposing sum of $50,000. for only ten days' work. Five
thousand dollars a day, or ten dollars a minute. That
means that he was being paid at the rate of twenty-five

W. C. FIELDS

His career started suddenly when he dropped a packing box on father's head

times as much per day for acting in Hollywood as the President gets for running the United States. Possibly you remember Mr. Dukenfield's masterly interpretation of the impecunious Micawber—because Claude William Dukenfield is, of course, the one and only, absolutely inimitable, W. C. Fields.

Seeing his name in flashing white lights is no novelty to the greatest juggler in the world. But on the other hand, being down in the gutter is no novelty to him either. At one time in his life, he didn't sleep in a bed for four whole years. He slept on park benches, in hallways, in packing boxes, and he slept even in holes in the ground with a strip of oilcloth for a blanket. He says that to this day, the greatest thrill life can offer him, is the luxury of stretching out at night between freshly laundered sheets.

When it comes to the precarious art of juggling. W. C. Fields has absolutely no equal anywhere in the world. He's been tossing and catching ever since he was fourteen years old. He started out by juggling apples and tennis balls in barns and blacksmith shops. He practised every day of his life, and sometimes for sixteen hours a day. He even practiced when he was so sick he could barely stand up.

His theory was that a juggler ought to be able to juggle anything he can lift, and today W. C. Fields can perform the most dazzling stunts with eggs, boards, hats, canes, frying pans, dishes, shoes, biscuits, cigars, bricks, candlesticks, and even flatirons.

He has juggled his way all around this awe-struck planet. He was applauded by the citizens of Johannesburg way back in the days of the Boer War. He was hissed by the patriots of Madrid right after the Spanish-American War. He convinced the good people of India,

Egypt, France, Germany, England and Australia that it's a cinch to juggle—if you know how.

Many people have the absurd notion that Fields is an Englishman. But that's not true. He was born in Pennsylvania, and he's as native to that state as Philadelphia scrapple.

W. C. Fields has been bumming around the world ever since he was a tow-headed kid of eleven. He ran away from home because of a misunderstanding with his father. At least, that's what he calls it today—a misunderstanding. His eyes light up and sparkle as he tells you about it. It all started rather suddenly over a shovel—a shovel that the boy had left lying on the ground. When Father Dukenfield stepped on the shovel, the shovel jumped up and barked his shins. He was hopping mad—but while he was hopping, he grabbed up the shovel and hit the boy a clip on the shoulder.

That blow was tempting fate. Young Claude felt he had been challenged.

So he got hold of a big box, dragged it into the house, climbed up on a chair, and balanced the box carefully on the top of the door. A few minutes later, when Father Dukenfield came in—*Wham!!*—down came the box and crowned him on the top of the head in the neatest slapstick tradition.

Then this astonishing brat did the most expedient thing possible—he took to his heels and ran as fast and as far as his skinny, long legs would carry him. He ran so fast and so far that he never went back again. And the next time he saw his father, little Claude Dukenfield was W. C. Fields, the greatest juggler on earth.

From the time he left home to the time he was sixteen, he was as homeless as a mongrel pup. He slept wherever he could find a corner to curl up, and he ate whatever food he could beg, borrow, or swipe. He snitched so many milk bottles from the porches of respectable houses that to this day, he shudders at the sight of a watch-dog. When you talk to W. C. Fields, you feel as though you were talking to someone who had truly stepped out of a Dickens' novel.

Once he was a professional drowner. He used to wade out into the ocean, roar for help, and pretend to flounder. Naturally, a crowd would gather to watch the rescue. And while Fields was gasping and sputtering for breath, his pals did a lively business selling hot dogs and ice cream to the onlookers. Sometimes, when business was brisk, he drowned as often as four or five times a day.

He was arrested more times than he can possibly remember, and he admits that if he tried the same things today, he'd land in a reformatory quicker than you can pull an ace out of a marked deck.

For a while he worked on an ice-wagon, and got up every morning at four o'clock. But all the while he was juggling, juggling with little pieces of ice and juggling with the ears of corn that he fed his horse.

After he'd been practising for two years, he answered a newspaper advertisement for a juggler, and got the job. The salary was five dollars a week, but he had to pay the greedy manager a dollar and a half a week as commission. So to save money, he slept in the dressing room and lived on pie at five cents a slice.

Then followed three whole seasons of work without pay. Of course, he was supposed to be paid, but something always went wrong. Either the show collapsed, or the manager ran off with the funds. But Fields took it philosophically—at least he ate three times a day, and slept in a real bed. After what he'd been through, that seemed like the life of Reilly.

Today, W. C. Fields has a fine house in Hollywood, and a private dressing room with fifty hats nailed to the ceiling. People stand in long lines outside of theatres all over the land to watch him go through those casual antics that it took him forty years to perfect. And he can sleep now every night between freshly laundered sheets.

For "To this day," he says, "when I climb between sheets, I *smile*. And when I get into bed and stretch out—*hot diggety*, is that a sensation!"

THERE has been only one author in the history of the world who ever wrote a book and made $49.49 profit on every single word in the book. That book was *The Specialist*, and its author was Chic Sale.

The Specialist was the first book Chic Sale ever wrote, and he had so little faith in it that he printed only two thousand copies at first; and it took six weeks to sell them. Then suddenly the book caught on and swept over the country like flames leaping and roaring through a pine forest. It sold more copies than *The Good Earth!*

You'd think, wouldn't you, that an author would be mighty proud of writing a book that outsold *The Good Earth?* But Chic Sale wasn't. He regretted that he ever wrote *The Specialist*—regretted it because its humor has been misunderstood by many people.

On the other hand, he was proud of the success it achieved. He was embarrassed when people spoke of the book in his presence, and preferred that no one mention it, especially if he thought the person considered the humor vulgar. Once his daughter actually wept because she felt the book had disgraced the family.

Chic Sale became an author more or less by accident. Actually, he was an actor and one of the finest character actors that ever put on grease paint.

For that matter, he became an actor more or less by accident too. Years ago, he was a mechanic, working in the railroad shops in Urbana, Illinois. His older sister

CHIC SALE

He couldn't sing; he couldn't dance; he was the best-known "horn player" in the United States, but he couldn't play a horn

had stage aspirations, so she went to Chicago and studied at a dramatic school. When she came home for Christmas vacation she gave a program at one of the churches and mimicked country characters.

After her performance was over, Chic said, "Why, I can do that without going to school."

She dared him to, so he walked out in the middle of the floor and gave an imitation of the local telegraph operator in Urbana. In a few minutes, he had the natives almost rolling off their chairs.

The next week a troupe of actors came to Urbana to put on a show. They had a comedy man who came out between the acts and entertained the audience, but he got sick. Chic Sale heard about it, and applied for the job.

The manager of the show was skeptical. But Chic gave him a sample of what he could do, and the manager took him on for the week, paid him ten dollars, and changed Chic's whole life.

Footlights! Glamour! The laughter of five hundred people! The applause of an audience! Why, a log chain and a span of Missouri mules couldn't have dragged him back to the machine shop after that.

Packing up his old telescope suitcase, he dashed off to Chicago, got a job on the stage and went to a cheap rooming house and began rehearsing his stunt. He decided that whiskers would make him look more like an old man; but he didn't know where he could buy them, so he took some hair stuffing out of his mattress, and made himself a set of whiskers out of horsehair. He used these mattress whiskers on the stage for eight months before he bought a real set of whiskers from a dealer in theatrical make-up.

His pay was very small, and every penny was precious. In order to keep himself from eating too much, he would buy cheap candy and nibble on it awhile before dinner.

This, most of the time, took the edge off his appetite.

Something hurt his stomach. Maybe it was this cheap candy. At any rate, he spent thousands of dollars for operations, and he carried a cook with him wherever he went because he couldn't eat hotel cooking. He also carried a steel trunk with him, a trunk made into a filing cabinet and filled with thousands of jokes! He had one of the world's largest collections of jokes, but he never told a funny story in a private conversation.

He played in six musical comedies on Broadway; but he couldn't sing and he couldn't dance. He was the best known "horn player" in the United States; yet he couldn't play a horn. He made $50,000. playing in shows that were about Paris; yet he never saw Paris.

He wore the same pair of shoes on the stage for sixteen years. They were the shoes he used when he played the parts of old men. He believed they brought him good luck, so he kept on repairing them and refused to have any others.

While playing in vaudeville, he fell in love with a girl from Missoula, Montana, an enchanting creature crowned with an aura of moonlight and flowering jasmine. He wasn't scared in the least when he faced a thousand people, in the theatre; but when he tried to propose to this girl, he stuttered and blushed and felt miserable. Saying he was ill, he left her and went to his hotel room.

When he got there, he proposed to her over the telephone. She accepted, they were married, and had four children.

After making so much money out of *The Specialist*, Chic Sale wrote another book. It was called: *The Corn Husker Crashes the Movies* and it didn't bring in enough cash to pay the printing bills!

WHAT THE MOVIES DIDN'T TELL ABOUT
THE BENGAL LANCER

ONE afternoon about ten years ago, a slim, serious young Englishman by the name of Yeats-Brown sat before my fireplace in Forest Hills and kept me spellbound for hours with tales of his adventures in the mystic and fabled lands of the East. He was thirty-nine years old then; and ever since he was nineteen, he had seen death on many battlefields.

He had been a prisoner of war in Bagdad and Constantinople. He had fought the Turks on the scorching hot desert sands of Mesopotamia, and he had fought the Germans on the muddy fields of Flanders. He had written a book entitled *The Bloody Years*, and yet, like Lawrence of Arabia, I found him a quiet, soft-spoken English gentleman more interested in poetry and philosophy than in fighting.

Yeats-Brown had little money to show for his twenty years of soldiering. He had no idea what the future held in store for him. But he didn't seem very much worried. Out there in the East, he had learned something of the calm philosophy of the Orient. He had become a disciple of mysticism and Yoga; he had studied under holy men and sought the secrets of the Vedanta.

He hadn't lived just one life like most of us. In his thirty-nine years, he had lived many lives—in fact, when

FRANCIS YEATS-BROWN

In a picture hat and a black fox fur, the police didn't
know him

he finally wrote the story of his hectic career in which he related many of the things he told me that afternoon, he called the book, *The Lives of a Bengal Lancer*. It was the sensational success of 1930. And it made one of the most engrossing films that ever came out of Hollywood. But, like most Hollywood films based on biographies, it deviated very, very far from the facts of Yeats-Brown's astonishing career.

Francis Yeats-Brown was only nineteen years old when he first put on the dashing blue and gold uniform and the blue and gold turban of the Royal Bengal Lancers—the proudest and lordliest cavalry in all the far-flung dominions of his Britannic Majesty. They were a picked body of men, the crack regiment of India, these Bengal Lancers. Their pay was almost nothing—something like ten dollars a month—and they had to supply their own horses and their own equipment. But they didn't go out there to Mother India for gain, these daring young men of England. They went there for glory—went out there embued with the spirit that carried Kitchener and Chinese Gordon and Sir Frances Drake and Sir Walter Raleigh to the ends of the earth.

They were up every morning at five o'clock and drilled for hours until the sun rose in the sky and the barrels of their guns became so hot they couldn't hold them any longer.

And, with the thermometer sizzling at one hundred degrees in the shade, they found their recreation tearing up and down the polo field. They were cut down by sun stroke and their bodies racked with malaria. But Yeats-Brown told me that the most dangerous and exciting sport in all India was "pig-sticking." That's what the English call it—"pig-sticking." Actually, it's galloping through forests of brambles and over rough, stony country hunting a wild boar with nothing but a bamboo pole with a spear stuck in the end of it.

No other animal in the world is so vicious as a wild boar that has been wounded. Three hundred pounds of bristling fury, sly as a fox, courageous as a lion, and as fast on his trotters as the swiftest cavalry horse. To fall within range of his razor-sharp tusks, means quick and certain death.

I asked Yeats-Brown to tell me of his narrowest escape from death. He said it occurred one day while he was out "pig-sticking." He and his men had flushed a great boar out of the brambles. The savage pig was racing across the field, his huge tusks glistening in the sun. Yeats-Brown, mounted on his polo pony, was in hot pursuit. Just as he drove his spear into the pig, his horse stumbled; and horse, pig and Yeats-Brown went down in a screaming, whinnying, helpless mass of tangled legs and clawing forefeet. Yeats-Brown was pinned under his kicking horse; the pig, impaled upon the spear, was struggling to get up. The horse heaved. And the pig got loose just as Yeats-Brown leaped to his feet and tore for the nearest tree. There he sat until a rescue party rode up. He had lost a tooth, sprained a thumb, and was bruised and mashed from head to foot. The pig was dead from his wounds. The only one who was completely happy was the horse, who ambled about nibbling grass with the unhurried leisure of the East.

But I suppose the strangest episode in Yeats-Brown's strange career was the time he disguised himself as a woman. He had been fighting the Turks out in Mesopotamia or "Mespot" as he called it. He had been taken prisoner by the Turks and had escaped from his vermin-infested cell in Constantinople, but had not been able to get out of the city. The Turkish authorities were searching for him frantically.

Naturally they were looking for an English officer, so they never suspected a German governess who used to meet a Russian prince in one of the cafés. The Russian Prince was also being watched by the authorities, but the sentimental Turks hadn't the heart to interfere with a little harmless flirtation. So when Yeats-Brown, all dolled up as a German governess, in a picture hat, with a veil, a black fox scarf around his shoulders and a muff over his hands, minced into the café, the Russian Prince would jump to his feet, bow respectfully and kiss the lady's hand. And the Turkish detectives would smile at one another knowingly and shrug their shoulders. After all, even a suspect Russian Prince was entitled to a little romance.

He was unable to get out of Turkey disguised as Mademoiselle Josephine, so he played another role. Overnight, he changed his sex and nationality and became a Hungarian mechanic who had lost his job in a munitions factory. He grew a small turned-up mustache and wore a derby hat, a pair of steel-rimmed glasses, a stained white vest, and a pair of shoes with elastic sides. Actually he looked like a second-rate comedian, but the Turks never doubted that he was the real McCoy.

Finally he was caught and thrown back into prison again. Once more he escaped by passing himself off as one of a crowd of Greeks who ate their supper in the prison garden. When they went out he went out with them, and walked down the street as calm and serene as the ever-living Buddha.

I asked him what was the most terrible sight he ever saw in all his years of fighting, and he told me this story.

When he was a prisoner of war, the Turks forced him to march two hundred miles to a prison camp; on the way, he marched through a town where there wasn't a single living inhabitant. The Turkish army had butchered a whole village of Armenians. The silence of death was everywhere, and the only living creatures were a few dogs slinking through the silent streets and the buzzards circling in the sky overhead.

A BORROWED BIRTH CERTIFICATE STARTED HER ON HER CAREER TO BE THE MOST FAMOUS WOMAN IN THE WORLD

WHO is the most famous woman in all the world? Frankly, I don't know. But my guess would be that the title goes to a little Canadian Irish girl who weighs only one hundred and three pounds and who was christened Gladys Marie Smith.

Miss Smith went on the stage when she was very young. Fortunately, she came under the friendly and expert tutelage of David Belasco; and that master showman changed the uninspiring name of Gladys Smith into something more elegant and euphonious. Belasco called her Mary Pickford.

Mary Pickford was a star when Greta Garbo was still rubbing lather on men's faces in a barber shop in Sweden. Her name was a household word long, long before Mae West was inviting us to come up and see her sometime.

She has been on the screen longer than any other motion picture star in the world. She was world-famous before Douglas Fairbanks stood, for the first time, in front of a camera. She was the highest-salaried player on the screen long before Charlie Chaplin ever saw Hollywood; she was lining 'em up at the box office before Tom Mix ever rode his first horse on to a motion picture lot.

MARY PICKFORD

She dried her wet handkerchiefs on the window pane
and spent ten cents a day for food

Mary Pickford was earning her living when she was so young that she had trouble with the child-labor laws. Organizations such as the Gary Society in New York tried to keep her from acting on the stage. They said she ought to be learning arithmetic at school instead of strutting about in the theatre. So Mary fooled them. She had a cousin who was a year older than she was; she used her cousin's birth certificate, and circumvented the minions of the law. That is why, to this day, *Who's Who* and other directories give her age as being one year older than it actually is.

Mary Pickford's grandfather was born on April 8th and her father also was born on April 8th. And by 1894 —which was the year of Mary's birth—it appears that April 8th had been sort of set aside by the Pickford family as a special day for bringing children into the world. So Mary's mother wanted to do what her mother-in-law had done. She wanted to give her husband a baby for a birthday present on April 8th. But, to everyone's dismay, little Mary's debut didn't quite come off on schedule time.

Mary, as a matter of fact, didn't arrive until 3:00 A.M. on April 9th; but the calendar and the clock were both ignored and her birthday was solemnly declared to be April 8th.

For more than a third of a century—or as long as her mother lived, the illusion was preserved, and the birthday continued to be celebrated on the 8th. But since her mother's death, Mary has grown more exact and now celebrates her birthday on April 9th.

Few careers offer such striking contrasts as Mary Pickford's.

At one time in her life, she did her own laundry, pasted her wet handkerchiefs on the window pane to dry and spent only ten cents a day for food. A dozen years later, she was making about $1,000. an hour or $15. a second.

In the old days when she was jobless and homeless, her mother used to scrape together a few pennies and make hash for the children; and hash is still one of Mary Pickford's favorite dishes. I have heard her say that she would rather have hash like her mother used to make than to dine on filet mignon or caviar.

How does the most famous woman in the world live? What does she do for pleasure?

Well, eating isn't one of her pleasures. I dropped in to see her one day about six o'clock in the evening and she told me the only thing she had eaten all day was one slice of toast and a cup of tea. I asked her if she was hungry and she said, "No, not at all."

Years ago, she read a book by Upton Sinclair called *The Jungle;* and she has never eaten much meat since. The mere sight of a butcher shop window makes her ill for hours, so she always closes her eyes when she has to pass one. As a child, she used to play with a pet lamb, and every time she sees roast lamb on the table now, the memories of her childhood make it impossible for her to eat it. She never eats pork; and she can't eat a fish that she has pulled out of the water herself; but she does eat fish that somebody else has caught.

Mary Pickford says that ambition is a curse. It drives you and possesses you and keeps you from doing the things you want to do. She likes to walk and ride horseback but she seldom has time to do either. She works from twelve to sixteen hours a day. She has two sets of secretaries, for she says she could never expect any secretary to work as hard or as long as she does.

She dislikes to waste a moment. She has a French traveling companion so she can polish up her French verbs even while she is traveling in her automobile.

She gets more mail than anyone else in the world. It would take her ten hours a day just to read her mail. The post office delivers it to her in great bags. She receives many begging letters. Her requests for money are ten times as great as her income.

Mary Pickford is real—the sort of person that you would love. Modest and sincere, she is totally unspoiled by any false ideas of her own importance. She told me she doesn't even care whether there is so much as a gravestone to mark her last resting place.

As everyone knows, she has often played children's parts on the screen; and the reason that she did it was because she longed to capture, in the world of illusion, some of the fairy delights of childhood that had been denied her.

I asked Miss Pickford if there weren't thousands of girls in America just as pretty and charming and capable as the stars in Hollywood. She said "Yes, of course. Success, however, depends so much upon opportunity, and opportunity is just another name for what we call 'the breaks.' So perhaps the stars in Hollywood are the persons with ability who got 'the breaks.'"

Mary's father was a purser on a lake steamer running between Toronto, Canada, and Buffalo, New York. He was killed when Mary was four years old by a freak accident—by bumping his head against an iron pulley. His name was John Smith. How astonished John Smith would be if he could come back and find his little Gladys the most famous woman in all the world!

Courtesy Warner Bros.

AL JOLSON
Hollywood paid him $6,000. a day for doing nothing

ONCE DOOMED TO DIE FOR WANT OF TEN CENTS—HE LIVED TO TEAR UP $1,000,000.

SO FAR as I know, there is only one actor in America who ever tore up a contract worth a million dollars.

You have seen him in pictures, you have sung his songs, you have laughed at his jokes. He made the first full-length talking picture. And he also made the greatest box-office attraction that was ever created in Hollywood —a picture that earned twelve million dollars, an all-time record that has never been approached by any other film.

That picture was *The Singing Fool*, and the man who starred in it was Asa Yoelson—Al Jolson to you.

Jolson once drew a salary of $31,250. a week and he drew it for more than six months without doing a day's work. That means he was paid almost a million dollars for doing absolutely nothing. To be sure, he was ready to perform; but his employers, United Artists, had no script ready to shoot just then; so he played golf and collected a salary that made the income of the President of the United States look like a stenographer's stipend.

Then he did one of the most unexpected and generous acts that has ever brightened the cynical darkness of Hollywood. The depression had just struck. Joseph Schenck, a life-long friend of Jolson's, had lost heavily. There was still more than a million dollars due Al Jolson on his contract; but he tore the contract up and handed it back to Joseph Schenck, head of United Artists, saying: "Forget it! I'm not doing anything for you and you don't need to pay me any more money."

Charles Schwab once created a sensation in Wall Street by tearing up a salary contract that guaranteed him a million dollars a year; but this once-poor actor tore up a contract that was paying him almost two million dollars a year. Nobody asked him to do it; nobody expected him to do it.

Al Jolson had tuberculosis when he was a boy. When he went to a free clinic at Bellevue Hospital for treatment, the doctors told him that if he didn't get away to the country at once, he would be dead in six months. The prescription they gave him was free, so was the medicine; but when he went to get it, he discovered that he had to pay ten cents for a bottle. He didn't have a dime—so to this day, he has never got the medicine.

He recovered without it, anyhow—and without the doctors. But he has never forgotten how it felt to be doomed to die because he didn't have ten cents. That is why he now spends twenty thousand dollars a year supporting free beds for poor people in a tuberculosis sanitarium in the Adirondacks at Saranac Lake. He has been doing this for eleven years; and he has never seen half of the people whose lives he has saved.

I'm often curious about people's birthdays; but when I asked Al Jolson when he was born, he said he didn't know. He thinks he is about forty-five or fifty; but he isn't positive. He was born of poor parents in Russia, born in a little hut with a straw roof and a stone floor. One year was about like another, and his parents didn't bother to keep track of a little thing like the birth of a child. So he hasn't the remotest idea whether he was born in 1885 or 1886 or 1888. But after he became famous, his friends wanted to give him birthday presents, so he had to pick out a birthday. He knew it would be bad business to be born in the autumn, for actors are always broke at the beginning of a season. But they are usually feeling pretty flush in the spring, and since May is a nice, warm month, he decided to be born in May—May 26, 1888. He admits that date is not accurate, but it is near enough. Anyhow, it can't be more than four or five years out of the way.

Jolson got his first job on the stage when he was a child—a small part in a play called *Children of the Ghetto*. He had just one line—he had to rush on to the stage and shout: "Kill the Jews!"

His father had a job just then slaughtering cattle in a kosher butcher shop during the week and singing in the synagogue on the Sabbath. So when he heard that his son was shouting in the theatre, "Kill the Jews!" young Jolson's career almost came to an abrupt end.

When Jolson first came to New York, he was penniless, and had to steal a ride from Washington. He was so unsophisticated that when he got to Newark, New Jersey, he thought he was in New York City; so he got off the train and had to sleep that night in a thicket of grass in the Jersey Meadows. When he awoke, his legs and hands were a mass of mosquito bites—raw, swollen, and bleeding.

When he finally got to New York, he slept on park benches and on trucks down by the water front. For days he went hungry. The best he could hope for then was a chance to "jump for nickels" in some Bowery saloon.

Lee Schubert once remarked that there were only two

legitimate actors in America who could go into any big town and fill a theatre on the strength of their names alone. One was Fred Stone, and the other was Al Jolson.

Yet Al Jolson told me that the first time he ever appeared at the Winter Garden, he was heartbroken. It was a long show, and he didn't go on until after midnight. He got no applause. Nothing. Not a ripple. That night, after the curtain was rung down, he stumbled up Broadway, sick with discouragement. He lived on Fifty-fourth Street, but he was so dazed that he walked all the way to Ninetieth Street—forty-six blocks out of his way —before he realized where he was!

And the furthest thing from his thoughts at that moment—from even his most delirious dreams—was that some day his name would flash like an aurora over Broadway, and that managers would leap at the chance of paying him ten dollars a minute!

SHAKESPEARE HAD A SHOT-GUN WEDDING

NO ONE paid much attention to him while he lived. A hundred years after his death his name was still practically unknown. Yet since that time millions of words have been written about him; he has aroused more comment than any other writer who ever sharpened his wisdom teeth on a goose-quill pen; and thousands of people, every year, make pilgrimage to the place where he was born.

I, for one, was there in 1921. I used to wander cross-country from Stratford to Slattery—treading the fields swept by his eager feet when, as an awkward country boy, he hurried to keep tryst with his sweetheart, Anne Whately.

Little did William Shakespeare suspect then that his name would ring down the centuries in a paeon of glory. And, fortunately, little did he suspect that his idyllic young love was doomed to sorrow—and to years of regret.

For there is no doubt about it—the tragedy of Shakespeare's life was his marriage. True, he loved Anne Whately—but late of moonlight nights he had been tempting fate with another lass, Anne Hathaway. When Anne Hathaway learned that her lover had taken out a license to wed someone else, she was stunned—she was crazed with fear. In desperation she rushed to the homes

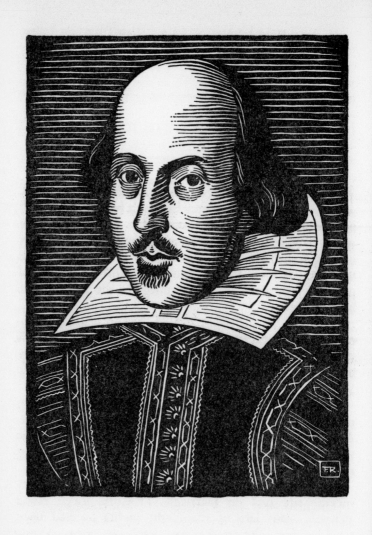

WILLIAM SHAKESPEARE

His home-town buried him with honors—because he was
a money-lender!

of her neighbors, and weeping with shame, explained why Shakespeare would have to marry her. Her neighbors—simple, honest-hearted yeomen—bristled with moral indignation. The very next day, they hurried to the town hall, and posted a bond for the marriage of Shakespeare to Anne Hathaway.

Shakespeare's bride was eight years older than himself —and from the very start, their marriage was a miserable farce. Time and again in his plays, he warns men against marrying older women—and as a matter of fact, he lived with Anne Hathaway very little of the time. Most of his married life was passed in London, and he probably returned to his family no oftener than once a year.

Today, Stratford-on-Avon is one of the loveliest towns in England—little thatched cottages, gardens of hollyhocks, quaint winding streets. But when Shakespeare lived there? It was dirty, poverty-stricken, and devastated by disease. There were no sewers. Pigs swarmed through the main streets devouring the garbage; and Shakespeare's father, one of the town officials, was fined for hoarding, outside his door, a pile of refuse from the stable.

We, in America, think we are having hard times now; but in Shakespeare's day, one half the population of Stratford was living on public relief. Most of the people were illiterate. Neither Shakespeare's father nor mother nor sister nor daughter nor grand-daughter could either read or write.

The man who was destined to become the power and the glory of English literature, had to leave school when he was thirteen and go to work. His father was a glovemaker and a farmer—and Shakespeare milked cows, sheared the sheep, churned the butter, and helped tan leather and soften hides.

But when he died, Shakespeare was a wealthy man by the standards of his day. Within five years of his arrival in London, he was making good money as an actor. He bought shares in two theatres, he dabbled in real estate, he lent money at a high rate of interest, and presently his income was three hundred pounds a year. The purchasing power of money then was about twelve times what it is today—so that when Shakespeare was forty-five, he had an income of something like $20,000. a year.

Yet how much money do you imagine he left his wife in his will? Not a cent. He left her nothing whatever except his second-best bedstead; and even that was an after-thought, for he wrote it in between the lines after the will had been drawn up.

Shakespeare had been dead seven years before all his plays were published in book form. Today, if you would like to buy a first edition, you can pick up a pretty excellent copy in New York for something like a quarter of a million dollars. Yet Shakespeare himself probably never got the equivalent of even six hundred dollars for such plays as *Hamlet*, *Macbeth*, or *A Midsummer Night's Dream*.

I once asked Doctor S. A. Tannenbaum, who has written a number of books on Shakespeare, if there was proof absolute that William Shakespeare of Stratford-of-Avon wrote Shakespeare's plays. And he answered that we are as certain of that as we are that Lincoln spoke at Gettysburg. Yet many people claim that Shakespeare didn't even exist, and dozens of books have been written to prove that his plays were really the work of Sir Francis Bacon, or the Earl of Oxford.

I have often stood in front of Shakespeare's grave, gazing down at that weirdest of all epitaphs:

Good frend for Iesus sake forbeare,
To digg the dust encloased here;
Bleste be ye man yt spares thes stones,
And curst be he yt moves my bones.

He was buried in front of the pulpit in the little village church; and why was he granted this place of honor? For his genius, which men still love these three hundred years later? Hardly. The poet who was destined to be the polestar of English literature was buried in the church because he lent money to his home town. If the man who created the character of Shylock hadn't lent money to his home town, his bones would today be forgotten in an unmarked grave.

ERNESTINE SCHUMANN-HEINK
They told her to go home and buy a sewing machine

HUNGRY, COLD AND DESPONDENT, SHE TRIED TO COMMIT SUICIDE AND LIVED TO BECOME ONE OF THE GREATEST SINGERS OF ALL TIME

THE story of how Madame Ernestine Schumann-Heink sang herself up to the golden aura of fame, in spite of hunger and heartbreak and despair is one of the most extraordinary tales in the whole lurid history of Grand Opera.

Her struggle for success was bitter and hard. She became so discouraged, so despondent, that she tried to commit suicide. Her marriage had proved to be a tragedy. Her husband had gone his way, leaving her saddled with his debts; and according to the German law in those days, a wife was responsible for her husband's debts. So the sheriff took away all her furniture, except a chair and a bed. When she got a job singing now and then, the sheriff took away most of her pay.

Six hours before her third child was born she was singing. She was in agony at the time; but she had to sing, because she had to feed her babies. When winter came, her children cried with hunger and shivered from cold, for she couldn't buy fuel to keep the bare room warm.

Half-insane with despair, she decided to kill herself and all of her children. . . .

But instead of committing suicide, she struggled on until she made herself one of the greatest contraltos in the world, and perhaps the most distinguished Wagnerian singer who ever thrilled an audience.

Some months before her death, she invited me to come and have dinner with her in Chicago, and promised to cook the dinner herself. Then she added, "If you tell me I am a great singer, I will like that; but if you have dinner with me and then say, 'Schumann-Heink, that is the best soup I ever ate,' then you will be a friend of mine forever."

She said that one of the secrets of her success as a singer was the fact that she loved people—and religion taught her to love. She read her Bible every day and used to get down on her knees and pray every night and morning.

She declared that even the tragedies of life had helped her singing, for they had given her understanding, sympathy, tenderness, and feeling. Her sufferings put a mystic something into her voice that thrilled the hearts of millions. If you ever heard her sing the Rosary in the hey-day of her glory, you must have felt that mysterious quality.

Knowing how intensely she loved children, I asked her why she tried to kill herself and her babies. Here is the story, as she told it to me.

"I was hungry and sick and depressed," she said, "And I saw no hope for the future. I didn't want my children to endure what I had gone through; I felt death would be better than that, so I determined to throw myself and my children in front of a train. I had planned it all out. I knew the time the train would pass. The children were crying and clinging to me, stumbling along at my side. I heard the train whistle. I was already near the tracks. I bent down to pull the children close together. I was ready to hurl their bodies and mine in front of the train when suddenly my little girl threw herself in front of me, crying, 'Mamma, I love you! It is so cold, please let us go home!'

"*Ach Gott!* That childish voice brought me to my senses. I grabbed all my children and ran back to our cold, bare room. I fell on my knees and prayed and sobbed my heart out."

Up to that time, practically everything Ernestine Schumann-Heink had undertaken in life had ended in futility—her marriage, her career. Yet within a few years after this attempt at suicide, the Royal Opera House in Berlin, Covent Garden in London, the Metropolitan in New York, were all bidding for her services. She had slaved and hungered for years. Then presto! Success came like a blinding flash, as it so often does.

Schumann-Heink's father was an Austrian officer. His pay was small, his family was large; so that even as a child Ernestine knew the pangs of hunger. She was thankful if she could get all the black bread she wanted to eat. Butter was a luxury unheard-of. Her mother skimmed the fat off the soup—when there was any fat to skim—and that was used in place of butter. When she went away to school, her lunch consisted of dry black bread and coffee; and at night she had dry black bread and soup —nothing else.

In order to get enough food to eat, she used to run away from school and go to a little menagerie on the edge of town and clean the monkey cages in return for a few sandwiches.

After years of study she was finally given an opportunity to sing for the director of the famous Imperial Opera Company in Vienna.

After listening to her sing songs that were destined to

make her famous, he told her that she would never be a singer, that she had no looks, no personality, and he advised her to go back home and buy a sewing machine and make dresses. "But an opera singer?" he cried, "*Ach, nein!* Never, never, never!"

Years later, after she had become world-famous, she sang in the Imperial Opera House in Vienna; and this same director congratulated her on her magnificent performance and said, "Your face looks familiar. Where have I seen you?"

"*Ha!*" said Schumann-Heink, "I told him! I said, '*Ja,* where you saw me? Right here's where you saw me! Remember?' And then I tell him about that sewing-machine . . . *Ja!*"

FIRED FROM FOUR NEWSPAPERS—HE WON THE NOBEL PRIZE AND THOUGHT IT WAS A GAG

MY FIRST encounter with Sinclair Lewis was years back. Years ago, he and I and a half-dozen other chaps used to hire a motor boat at Freeport, Long Island, and chug out a few miles to fish for mackerel or weakfish. In those days, I took my hat off to Red Lewis because he never got seasick. The waves would toss and the sea would pitch, and down I would go to the bottom of the boat; but Lewis just sat up straight and kept on fishing like a man on a painted ocean.

Today I take my hat off to Sinclair Lewis, not for his skill as a fisherman (I can stay on deck myself now) but because he has written an unceasing stream of excellent novels. And if you don't think that's a man's job—try it!

Sinclair Lewis hit the bull's eye for the first time in 1920. Previous to that, he had written six books without causing a literary ripple. His seventh novel was *Main Street* and it swept over the nation like a tornado. Women's clubs condemned it, preachers denounced it, and newspapers called it an insult to American life. It raised a veritable literary war here; and the repercussions of it were heard three thousand miles away in Europe.

That book made him a literary star of the first magnitude.

SINCLAIR LEWIS

He wrote night and day for six months—then he sold
a joke for $2.

Some of the critics said: "Well, that's fine; but that smart aleck will never be able to do it again."

Oh, no?

The red-headed boy from Sauk Center, Minnesota, set to work; and since then he has—well, I was about to say he has "dashed" off half a dozen best sellers. But Sinclair Lewis doesn't dash off his books. He works over them, constantly revising and rewriting.

He wrote an outline of sixty thousand words for his novel *Arrowsmith*. That means that the mere outline was more than half as long as the average novel. He worked for twelve months once on a novel about capital and labor and then tossed the manuscript into the waste-paper basket.

He started to write *Main Street* three different times. He started it exactly seventeen years before he finished it.

Main Street was followed by a whole series of books that leaped instantly into the best-seller class. *Babbitt—Arrowsmith—Elmer Gantry—Dodsworth—Ann Vickers—It Can't Happen Here*. . . .

I once asked Sinclair Lewis to tell me the most astonishing fact he knew about himself. He thought a moment and then said that if he weren't doing literary work, he would prefer either to teach Greek or Philosophy in Oxford University—or go out to the deep woods and live with a bunch of lumber jacks.

For six months out of the year, he loves to live on swanky Park Avenue; but during the other six months, he lives in an isolated spot in the Vermont mountains, eighty miles southeast of Burlington. He has a three-hundred-and-forty-acre farm up there covered with sugar trees and he makes his own maple syrup and raises his own vegetables. And he "goes in to town" only when he needs a hair-cut.

I asked, "Red, how does it feel to be famous?"—and he replied, "Oh, it's a nuisance." He told me that if he answered all his mail, he not only would never be able to write another book, but he wouldn't even have time to sleep. So he just chucks most of his letters into the fireplace and watches them burn.

He dislikes autograph hunters, seldom goes to public dinners, and shuns literary teas.

When I began talking about his early struggles, he said, "Oh, these writers that are always talking about their early struggles give me a pain. The trouble with most American writers is that they don't have enough struggles. They don't have any more trouble getting started than do young dentists and doctors and lawyers; but they are more articulate and they like to talk about what a hard time they have had."

I reminded him of the fact that for years he used to get up a couple of hours before breakfast and go out to the kitchen and put the coffee on to boil and write on the kitchen table. I reminded him that he once borrowed a hundred and fifty dollars and did his own cooking and washing and worked night and day for six months, and the only thing that he sold during all that time was one joke for two dollars. But he said there was no hardship to that, he said he was merely learning his trade and he never had a better time in his life than he did during those years.

I asked him how many copies of his books had been sold, and he said he didn't know. I said, "Well, now, come, you can give me even an approximate figure, can't you?" And he said, "No, I haven't the slightest idea."

I asked him how much money he made out of *Main Street*. He told me that he didn't know and he really didn't care. He said he had an attorney and an accountant to look after his business affairs, and he never paid any attention to how much money he was making.

He has had all sorts of experiences. His father was a country doctor on the prairies of Minnesota and Sinclair Lewis sometimes gave a patient chloroform while his father performed an operation. He once worked his way across the Atlantic Ocean on a cattle boat and he once traveled in the steerage down to Panama to get a job. He used to write children's poetry, he used to sell plots for stories to Jack London, and he used to be assistant-editor of a magazine for deaf people.

He doesn't take any exercise whatever. He agrees with George Jean Nathan that opening the door of a taxicab and crawling inside is all the exercise a city man needs.

He has no interest whatever in sports. Babe Ruth is the only baseball player he can name, and Red Grange is the only football player he ever heard of.

"You were fired from the first three newspapers you worked for, weren't you?" I asked.

"No. I was fired from the first *four* papers I worked for," was his reply.

I wanted to ask him what advice he would give to young writers and I began, "What advice . . ." and he said— "None." He doesn't believe in giving anybody any advice about anything.

One day somebody with a Swedish accent telephoned him saying that he had been awarded the Nobel Prize for literature. Sinclair Lewis had known a lot of Swedes out in Minnesota, and he thought this fellow's accent was a bit phony; Red supposed some friend was playing a joke on him and he began to kid the fellow.

A few minutes later, Lewis was flabbergasted when he discovered that it was all real—that he really had won the greatest distinction in the literary world!

JOHN D. ROCKEFELLER
He used to get four cents an hour for hoeing potatoes

SHE TURNED HIM DOWN BECAUSE
HE HAD "NO PROSPECTS"—HIS
NAME WAS JOHN D.

JOHN D. ROCKEFELLER did three astonishing things:

First, he amassed probably the greatest fortune in all history. He started out in life hoeing potatoes under the boiling sun for four cents an hour. In those days, there were not half a dozen men in all the United States who were worth even one million dollars; but John D. managed to amass a fortune estimated at anywhere from one billion to two billion dollars.

And yet the first girl he fell in love with refused to marry him. Why? Because her mother said she was not going to let a daughter of hers "throw herself away" on a man who had such poor prospects as John D. Rockefeller.

The second astonishing thing that Mr. Rockefeller did was this, he gave away more money than anyone else has done in all history.

He gave away $750,000,000—and that means that he gave away seventy-five cents for every minute that has passed night and day since the birth of Christ—or to put it another way, John D. gave away six hundred dollars for every day that has dawned since Moses led the children of Israel across the Red Sea, three thousand five hundred years ago.

And the third astonishing thing about Rockefeller was that he lived to be ninety-seven. He was one of the most bitterly hated men in America. He received thousands of letters from people threatening to kill him. He had to be protected day and night by armed bodyguards. He endured the terrific nervous and physical strain of building up and managing all his far-flung enterprises.

The strain of business killed Harriman, the railroad builder, at sixty-one.

Woolworth founded his vast chain of five-and-ten-cent stores and was done with life at sixty-seven.

"Buck" Duke made a hundred million dollars out of tobacco and died at sixty-eight.

But John D. Rockefeller made a far greater fortune than Woolworth, Duke and Harriman all put together. And remember, only thirty white men in a million ever reach the age of ninety-seven—and there is probably not one man in a hundred million who ever reaches ninety-seven without needing artificial teeth. But John D. at ninety-seven hadn't a false tooth in his head.

What was the secret of his long life? He probably inherited a tendency to live long. And this tendency was strengthened by a calm, placid disposition. He never got excited and he was never rushed.

When he was head of the Standard Oil Company, he had a couch in his office at 26 Broadway; and come what might, he had a half-hour's nap everyday at noon. And he continued to take five naps a day until his death.

When John D. Rockefeller was fifty-five, he had a physical breakdown. That was one of the happiest accidents that ever happened in the whole history of medicine; for because of his own illness, John D. was stimulated to give millions to medical research. As a result of his ill health, the Rockefeller Foundation is spending almost a million dollars a month to promote health throughout the world.

I was in China during the terrible cholera epidemic of 1932, and in the midst of all that poverty and ignorance and disease I was able to walk into the Rockefeller Medical College at Peking and get a vaccination for cholera. Never until then had I realised how much Rockefeller was doing for suffering humanity in Asia and the remote corners of the earth. The Rockefeller Foundation has tried to stamp out hookworm all over the world; it is waging a winning battle against malaria; and its physicians discovered a vaccine for the dreaded yellow fever.

John D. earned his first dollar by helping his mother raise turkeys and until his death he kept a flock of fine turkeys on his eight thousand acre estate—kept them to remind him of the scenes of his childhood.

He saved all the nickels his mother paid him for tending turkeys and stored the money in a cracked teacup which he kept on the mantel piece. He worked on a farm for thirty-seven cents a day and saved all his wages until he accumulated fifty dollars. Then he lent those fifty dollars to his employer at seven per cent interest and discovered that his fifty dollars could make as much for him in a year as he could earn by ten days of gruelling work.

"That settled it," he said. "I determined then and there to let money be my slave instead of being the slave of money."

John D. didn't spoil his son with too much money. For example, he gave him a penny for each fence post he could find on the estate that needed to be repaired. He found thirteen in one day, and was paid thirteen cents. Then John D. paid his son fifteen cents an hour for repairing fences, and his mother gave him five cents an hour for practising on the violin.

John D. never went to college. He finished high school and attended a commercial school for a few months. He was through with academic study forever when he was sixteen; yet he gave fifty million dollars to the University of Chicago.

He was always intensely interested in the church. As a young man he taught Sunday school classes, never danced, never played cards, never went to the theatre and didn't smoke and didn't drink.

He said grace before each meal and he had the Bible read to him daily—and in addition, he also had read to him selections from a book of poems and prayers containing uplift messages for every day.

The Rockefeller fortune is still growing at the approximate rate of one hundred dollars a minute, yet Mr. Rockefeller's only great ambition was to round out a century of life; and he said that if he were alive on his hundredth birthday—July 8, 1939—he was going to lead a band on his estate at Pocantico Hills. And the tune they were going to play was: *When You and I Were Young, Maggie*.

HE WENT TO SCHOOL FOR ONLY FOUR
YEARS—YET HE WROTE SEVENTEEN
IMMORTAL NOVELS

NINETY years ago, and just about Christmas time, a little book was published in London—a story destined to become immortal. Many people have called it "the greatest little book in the world." When it first appeared, friends meeting each other on the Strand or Pall Mall asked, "Have you read it?" and the answer invariably was, "Yes, God bless him, I have."

The day it was published a thousand copies were sold. Within a fortnight, the presses had dashed off fifteen thousand copies. Since then, it has been whirled into countless editions and has been translated into almost every language under heaven. A few years ago, J. P. Morgan purchased the original manuscript for a fabulous price; and it now reposes among his other priceless treasures in that magnificent art gallery in New York City which he calls his library.

What is this world-famous book? Charles Dickens' *Christmas Carol.*

Charles Dickens was destined to become the most prolific and best-loved author in English literature; yet when he first started writing, he was so afraid of being laughed at that he sneaked out and mailed his first manuscript in the dead of night so that nobody would discover his audacity.

CHARLES DICKENS

The idol of the English-speaking world; yet his own
home was filled with heartbreak

He was twenty-two years old then, and when his story was actually printed, he was so overjoyed that he wandered aimlessly around the streets with the tears streaming down his face.

He wasn't paid a cent for that story. And his next eight stories netted him—how much do you suppose? Nothing. Absolutely zero. When he finally did get paid real money for a story, he received a check for the royal sum of five dollars. Yes, his first story brought him only five dollars; but his last manuscript brought his estate fifteen dollars a word—the highest price ever paid to an author since the beginning of time! Fifteen dollars a word! Why that is precisely fifteen times as much as Calvin Coolidge and Theodore Roosevelt were ever paid.

Most authors are ignored and forgotten within five years after their death. But sixty-three years after Dickens' death, publishers paid his estate more than a fifth of a million dollars for the story of our Lord—a little book that Dickens had written for his own children.

During the last hundred years, the novels of Charles Dickens have had a phenomenal sale. They have been outsold only by Shakespeare and the Bible. They have been perennial favorites, both on the stage and on the motion picture screen.

Charles Dickens never went to school more than four years in all his life; yet he wrote seventeen of the greatest novels in the English language. His parents ran a school, but he never went to it. Why? Because it was a school for young ladies. Or at least, it was supposed to be. A brass plate bearing the words, "Mrs. Dickens' Establishment," hung outside the front door for a whole year; but in the whole of London, there was not even one young lady who came there to be educated.

The bills kept mounting and soaring. The creditors

pleaded and swore and pounded the table. Finally, in a
fit of holy indignation, they had Dickens' father flung
into jail for debt.

Charles Dickens' childhood was sordid and pathetic.
It was more than that—it was tragic. He was only ten
years old when his father was thrown into prison, and
the family had nothing to eat; so every morning, Charles
went to the pawnshop and sold some of the few remaining pieces of household furniture. He even had to sell
his dearly beloved books—ten of them—the only companions he had really ever known. In later years he
said, "When I sold my books, I thought my heart would
break."

Finally Mrs. Dickens took four of her children and
went to live with her husband in prison. At sun-up,
Charles went to the prison and spent the whole day there
with his family. And at night, he tramped back to the
dismal attic room where he slept with two other boys—
gutter-snipes from the slums of London. They made his
life a veritable hell. Finally he got a job pasting labels on
bottles of blacking in a rat-infested warehouse. With
the first few pennies he earned, he rented another room,
a dark little hole in an attic with a heap of dirty bedding
flung in the corner; yet Dickens said that little hole in an
attic was "like a Paradise" to him.

In later years, Dickens, the writer, avenged his own
childhood by creating the unforgettable portrait of
Oliver Twist holding out his empty porridge bowl and
asking for more.

Dickens wrote vivid scenes of perfect domestic bliss.
Yet his own marriage was a failure—a dismal, tragic failure. He lived for twenty-three years with a wife he
didn't love. She bore him ten children. But year by year
his misery deepened. He had the whole world fawning

at his feet; but his own home was filled with heartbreak. Finally the misery became so sharp, so poignant, that he could no longer endure it. So he did an unheard-of thing in those Victorian days—he published an announcement in his own magazine declaring that he and his wife had separated. Did he shoulder the blame himself? He did not. He tried to throw it all on her.

Dickens was considered the soul of generosity. When he died, he left a fifth of a million dollars to his sister-in-law, but how much did he leave to the mother of his own children? Thirty-five dollars a week!

He was as vain as a Siamese peacock. The slightest word of criticism sent him into a towering rage. He was proud of his striking appearance and when he first came to America in 1842, he dazzled the populace with his scarlet vests and robins'-egg-blue overcoats. He shocked Americans by combing his hair in public, and Americans shocked and horrified him by letting their pigs run loose around the streets of New York City.

Dickens was the best-loved and most idolized man of his day. On his second visit to America, people stood in line for hours, shivering in the wind, while waiting to buy tickets. In Brooklyn, people lighted bonfires and lay all night on mattresses in the street, risking frost-bite and pneumonia for the privilege of paying three dollars apiece to hear him talk. And when the tickets were sold out and hundreds had to be turned away, his admirers actually started a riot.

The history of literature is packed with contradictory characters, but taken all in all, Charles Dickens is about the most astonishing of the lot.

KATHERINE HEPBURN

Father taught her to throw a man weighing 180 pounds

$10,000. FOR ONE DAY'S WORK—YET
SHE CROSSES IN THE STEERAGE

ONE night not so many years ago, a scrawny, red-headed little girl in Connecticut strode confidently on to her school platform to recite *The Battle of Blenheim*. Her freckled face was scrubbed clean. In the audience sat her mother and father, her five brothers and sisters, all beaming with anticipation. It was to be a big occasion. Then something sad happened. As little Katie opened her mouth to say the opening lines, she was struck dumb with stage fright. She choked and gasped; tears welled up in her eyes; and finally in utter disgrace, she turned and fled from the platform.

Katherine Hepburn was only thirteen years old then. At just twice that age, she was winning medals for her outstanding performances in moving pictures—in 1933, for her work in *Morning Glory*; in 1934, for *Little Women*.

Not long after Katie left Bryn Mawr, the gods were good to her. After only two weeks' experience on the stage, she was handed the leading role in a Broadway production called *The Big Pond*. It was an extraordinary break. But when she began rehearsing for the play, she argued with the stage director about how she ought to play her part. She argued, but he had the last word—and she found herself out of a job.

Next she was given an important role in *Death Takes a Holiday*. But she never even got to Broadway with that play. She was fired in Philadelphia, fired while she was sitting in her dressing-room putting on her make-up and getting ready for a performance—fired for sheer incompetence.

Still another golden opportunity fell into her lap. She was given a role opposite Leslie Howard in *The Animal Kingdom*. She was desperately eager to make good. So for months she studied and lived and dreamed the part. But when rehearsals began, it was the same old story over again. She scorned all advice, insisted upon playing the role as she saw it—and again down came the axe and she was through.

Foolish? Well, before we condemn her, let me give you her explanation. Katherine Hepburn says: "I believed that if I could express myself in my own individual way, I would succeed. I knew that if I followed the blind dictates of other people my work would lack the vital spark and I would fail." And of course, she was right, dead right.

Years before this, her father, a physician in Hartford, Connecticut, had built a gymnasium in his home and had trained all six of his children to wrestle and tumble and perform on the flying trapeze. Katie became so dextrous that she could throw a man weighing a hundred and eighty pounds, and hold him down on the floor—although she herself was a bantam-weight of only one hundred and ten. She became a fancy skater, and a fancy diver, and her golf is so good that she nearly took it up as a career instead of acting. All this training helped her to make good in her first big Broadway hit as the leaping Amazon in *The Warrior's Husband*. And what a lively Amazon she made!

Her performance was so striking that Hollywood heard about her, gave her a screen test, and sent her a telegram asking how much salary she wanted. Hollywood thought she would ask two hundred or possibly two hundred and fifty a week. So when her agent wired the Hollywood executives that Miss Hepburn would be willing to come for *fifteen hundred* a week, they thought it was a typographical error. They wired to the agent and asked if the telegraph company hadn't added an extra cipher by mistake.

Back came the answer, stinging hot: "No. I am the one that made the mistake. Fifteen hundred a week is too little."

When Katie arrived in Hollywood, George Cukor who was going to direct her, told her that she needed a haircut, and that her clothes were a disgrace.

A disgrace? Katie gasped. "What do you mean!" she said. "Why, I had these clothes made especially for me by one of the finest houses in Paris."

"Well," George Cukor snapped back, "I think they're the worst-looking clothes I ever saw in my life. No well-dressed woman would wear them outside of a bathroom!" Katie choked. Then she started to laugh.

Katherine Hepburn spent four years at Bryn Mawr studying to be a psychologist. Feminine frills and fripperies never seemed important to her. She shocked Hollywood by going around in patched blue overalls and hobnailed shoes—great thick heavy shoes that she had worn when climbing mountains in Europe.

She has greenish blue eyes, and red hair; and when she is working on a picture, she has her hair shampooed every morning to give it a fiery tinge.

Once when she was dancing at college, a young man bumped into her; and when he turned to apologize, she withered him with a look of wrath. He was intrigued. During the next dance, he cut in, got acquainted with her, and asked her for a date. There were drives in the moonlight, talk of love; and in six months, they were married. Later, they were divorced in Yucatan. The only explanation Katie gave was a simple one: "It seemed like the best thing to do," she said.

She has made seven trips to Europe in the steerage; and she made one trip in the steerage even after Hollywood had paid her fifteen hundred a week. She doesn't like to waste good money on a first-class passage when she is positive before-hand that she is going to be so sick that she doesn't know whether she is traveling in a ship or on a Shetland pony.

She's a sharp girl when it comes to a bargain. After she had finished the picture *Spitfire,* and fulfilled her part of the contract, it was discovered that another scene had to be made. She was called back; and it is said on good authority that for one day's additional work, she received the tidy little sum of ten thousand dollars. She is probably the only girl in history who ever did that. And as one Scotsman to another, Katie—congratulations!

HE OFFERED A MILLION DOLLARS
FOR A BRIDE

DIAMOND JIM BRADY, the Haroun Al Raschid of
Broadway, died during the World War; and his
passing robbed the Great White Way of one of its most
incredible phenomena. While he lived, Brady threw the
wildest parties this weary old world has seen since the
days when the old Roman Emperors dined on the
nightingales' tongues. Sometimes he had as many as five
parties whooping it up all at once in five different parts
of the town. Sometimes these parties lasted for seventeen
riotous hours, and cost as high as a hundred thousand
dollars. He was fond of presenting his guests with
souvenirs to take home with them—little knick-knacks
and mementoes, such as diamond brooches or diamond
watches worth a thousand dollars apiece.

Diamond Jim, the Good-time Charlie of Broadway,
was born in a cheap flat above a saloon which his father
kept on the waterfront in New York; he learned to pop
the cork out of a bottle before he learned his *Mother
Goose*. Yet he himself never drank a drop of liquor in
his life. During the years when he reigned supreme on
Broadway, he squandered hundreds of dollars on liquor,
buying more champagne and Rhine wine than any other
man in the Western Hemisphere, but he gave it all to his
friends. While they drank themselves under the table,

JIM BRADY
5,000 handkerchiefs; 200 suits; 2,548 diamonds; 19 rubies;
no alcohol

Diamond Jim sat by and quenched *his* inconsequential thirst on fourteen or fifteen steins of root beer.

He weighed two hundred and fifty pounds, and loved to eat. He devoured a fifteen-course dinner every night with usually two or three helpings of all the main courses. Then he would eat a pound of chocolates and take a box of peppermints along to the theatre. He sent hundreds of boxes of candy to his friends each week. His candy bill alone averaged between two and three thousand dollars a month. He detested tea and coffee, but he had a passion for orange juice. He drank a whole gallon of orange juice before he even tucked a napkin under his bottom-most chin, and he often guzzled another whole gallon with his meal. Once he ate six chickens at one sitting. This sounds fantastic, but in his old age, when he underwent an operation, the doctors discovered that he had a stomach six times the normal size.

How did Diamond Jim Brady make his millions? He was one of the most expert salesmen that this high-pressure country ever produced. Besides, he was lucky. He got the breaks. He started selling steel cars in the early days when the railroads were equipped with wooden coaches. The country was expanding. Railroads were being flung like lariats from ocean to ocean and from Canada to the Gulf.

When he first started selling steel cars, they were still an experiment. No one wanted them. So he was given what turned out to be a phenomenal contract. This contract gave him 33⅓% commission on every car sold. Presently every railroad in the nation was clamoring for steel cars. And they had to come, hat in hand, to Diamond Jim Brady to get them, for at that time he had no competitors. So he made twelve million dollars selling steel cars. He was a product of his age. If he had been born fifty years later and tried selling steel cars today, he might not have been able to pay his grocery bill.

Diamond Jim made himself famous from Skowhegan to Santa Fé by one of the weirdest publicity stunts ever heard of since the days of Barnum. He literally *bedecked* himself with diamonds. He owned a different set of jewelry for every day in the month, and he frequently changed his jewelry as often as six or seven times a day. He used to ramble down Broadway bespangled with no less than two thousand, five hundred and forty-eight scintillating diamonds—and nineteen rubies. He wore priceless shirt-studs made to represent bicycles and automobiles, and cuff-links made like locomotives and freight cars.

He went to preposterous lengths to spend his money. He had a farm in New Jersey where, on gala occasions, the cows were milked into pails heavily plated with gold. His billiard table was inlaid with carnelians and lapis lazuli. His poker chips were made of onyx and mother-of-pearl. He paid an interior-decorator a third of a million dollars to furnish his house, and every year he gave away all his furniture to his friends and bought himself new furnishings.

He presented Lillian Russell with a bicycle plated with gold and studded all over with hundreds of diamonds, rubies, sapphires and emeralds. And when the shapely Lillian pedaled *that* bike up Fifth Avenue—well, things happened to the traffic!

Diamond Jim owned five thousand handkerchiefs and two hundred suits of clothes, and he never permitted himself to be seen in public without a Prince Albert and a tall silk hat. Even if he was only riding a handcar down a stretch of Western track with no one but prairie dogs to see him, Diamond Jim still wore his Prince Albert coat and his stovepipe hat and carried his diamond-studded cane.

Diamond Jim's stomach was six times its normal size, then so was his heart. For years, he lent money with a lavish hand to almost everyone who came to him with a hard-luck story. He knew he would never get most of it back, but he didn't mind. "It's fun to be a sucker," he said, "—if you can afford it."

When he knew that he was going to die, he discovered that he held notes and I.O.U.'s for a fifth of a million dollars; and one of the last things he ever did was to destroy every note in his possession, just to make sure that his executors wouldn't try to collect them.

"If I'm gonna die," he said, "I'm gonna die. But I ain't gonna leave trouble and heartache behind me."

When he died, he left practically all of his great fortune to charity. His diamonds and rubies and emeralds were estimated to be worth two million dollars. These were taken out of their settings and put into rings and sold again; so that many a woman today, without suspecting it, is wearing a stone that once enhanced the expansive charms of Diamond Jim.

Everyone "loved" Diamond Jim, yet he always remained a bachelor. He laid a million dollars in Lillian Russell's lap and asked her to marry him, but she refused. And once he said, "There ain't a woman in the world would marry an ugly-lookin' guy like me," and he laid his head on the table and cried like a baby.

HETTY GREEN

She owned two railroads outright, but sat up all night in
the day coach

AT ONE time, Hetty Green was the richest woman in America. At her death, she was worth at least $65,000,000. possibly $100,000,000. Yet almost any scrubwoman wears finer clothes than Hetty Green wore, eats a better dinner, and sleeps in a better bed.

Her income was $5. a minute, or $300. an hour; yet she would buy a morning newspaper for two cents, read it, and then have it sold again.

On cold winter days, she often padded herself with newspapers to keep warm. She bought a couple of railroads outright—bought them lock, stock, and barrel— and she owned bonds of almost every railroad in the country; yet when she was taking a train journey, she never indulged in the luxury of a Pullman berth, but sat up all night in the day coach.

Once she invited her friends to meet her at the Parker House in Boston for a dinner party. Everyone expected it to be quite an affair. Ladies appeared in their evening wraps, and the gentlemen wore dinner coats. But after her guests had arrived, Hetty led them out of the hotel and walked them a long distance to a cheap boarding house and treated them to a twenty-five cent dinner.

Sometimes when she was in Boston, she ate at a restaurant in Pie Alley—a place where one could get a plate of beans for three cents and a small wedge of pie for two cents. Her income then was more than eight cents every second. That meant she would have had to eat four pieces of pie every second just to keep up with her income.

When she was seventy-eight years old, a newspaper reporter asked her the secret of her good health. She said that she ate a tenderloin steak, fried potatoes, a cup of tea and some milk every morning for breakfast and then chewed baked onions all day to kill the germs that were in the steak and the milk. Unfortunately, she didn't say what she chewed to kill the germs in the onions.

On a sizzling hot day in 1893, Hetty Green crawled up into the attic of a warehouse that she had inherited from her father. The July sun boiled down upon the iron roof and made the attic just a trifle less hot than the outskirts of Hades. Yet Hetty Green worked in that devastating heat for hours. . . . Doing what? . . . Sorting white rags from colored ones because the junk man paid a cent a pound more for white rags!

She had to spend most of her time in Wall Street looking after her investments. That was dangerous, and she knew it. She realized that if she rented an apartment in New York City, or owned even one stick of furniture in the state, the tax collector would swoop down upon her and take $30,000. from her every year. So, to dodge tax collectors, she drifted about from one cheap lodging house to another. Even her best friends didn't know where she was hiding half the time. She lived under assumed names, dressed in rags, and carried so little baggage that suspicious landladies often made her pay for her night's lodging in advance.

As she grew older, a miracle happened. A friend persuaded her to spend $300. for beauty treatments. Each treatment was guaranteed to make her look one year younger.

Always fearing that some crook would forge her signature to a check, she never signed her name unless she had to. She saved all the envelopes that came addressed to her through the mails, and wrote her messages on the back of these envelopes. That relieved her of the necessity of signing her own name.

A friend of mine, Boyden Sparkes, is the co-author of a biography called *Hetty Green, A Woman Who Loved Money*. He told me that Hetty Green used to keep several million dollars on deposit at the Chemical National Bank in New York, and so she made herself at home there. She left her trunks and suitcases in the bank and she kept her old dresses and dusty rubbers in the vault. She brought an old one-horse buggy to the bank, took the wheels off, and had it stored on the second floor; and when she gave up her apartment in Hoboken, she stored her furniture in the bank.

Yet, in many ways, she had a kindly heart. For example, there was a porter at the bank, an old fellow who washed windows and ran errands and looked like a tramp. One day the bank fired him, and Hetty Green felt so sorry for him that she spent almost a week of her time getting him another job.

She died at the age of eighty-one from a stroke of paralysis, and the nurses who cared for her during her last illness were not permitted to wear their white uniforms. They wore street dresses so that Hetty would think they were ordinary servants—for the old lady could not have died peacefully had she suspected that they were expensive, trained nurses.

THEODORE DREISER
They wouldn't give him a job, so he just sat in the office
until they gave in

GOD'S MERCY AND THREE GIN RICKEYS BROUGHT A TITAN TO AMERICAN LITERATURE

THEODORE DREISER is one of the most astonishing novelists in America—and one of the most distinguished. For a third of a century, he has been on a literary rampage, bellowing and snorting and pawing up the earth like a short-horn bull.

He has had an immense influence upon American literature. The books you are reading today would have been a trifle different if Theodore Dreiser had never lived.

In 1900, he wrote a sensational novel called *Sister Carrie*, which stirred up a tornado of talk. Critics denounced it as immoral and obscene. Preachers pounded their pulpits and women's clubs rose up in holy indignation and demanded that it be suppressed. The publisher became frightened, and refused to sell it. Dreiser was astonished. He didn't know there was anything immoral about his novel. He had only depicted life as he saw it. But that was in 1900. Nobody would think of denouncing the book now. And if you want a copy of the first edition of *Sister Carrie* today, it will cost you $350. I once went up to see this grey, glum, gruff giant. He is so frank he makes you gasp.

When he goes to parties, he is something of a problem, for he tells people precisely what he thinks. For example

—at one party he got in an argument about Russia with one of the best-known bankers in New York. He accused the banker of being a fool and called him a bandit. Dreiser says he is not going to stand for any hooey.

He has written the most moving tragedies ever penned about American life. His greatest book, *An American Tragedy*, appeared in 1925, when the author was so hard up he could hardly pay his room rent. The book created a national sensation and four hundred thousand dollars came roaring down upon him like an avalanche. Hollywood paid him almost a fifth of a million dollars for the movie rights alone. I asked him what he did with the money—he put it in stocks, bonds and mortgages, and lost $300,000.

Dreiser writes about life in the raw because that is the way he was brought up in Terre Haute, Sullivan, Evansville and Warsaw, Indiana. His mother took in washing, and tried to feed thirteen children, but little Theodore sometimes went hungry and he often went cold. There was no bed for him to sleep on, so he curled up like a dog on a straw mattress on the floor. Sometimes he picked up little chunks of coal along the railway to keep the house warm. At times, he couldn't go to school because he didn't have shoes.

When he did attend school, he was a sort of dunce because he refused to study the things he was supposed to study. He hated mathematics and he despised grammar. He told me that he never studied grammar and never intended to study it. He vowed that if he had his way, he would abolish all classes in grammar and English literature, all courses in short story writing, and all schools of journalism. He says you can't make writers that way.

Dreiser suddenly decided one day that he was going to

be a newspaper reporter, so he applied for a job on the *Chicago Globe*. They told him they didn't need any help. But he took a chair and said he was going to sit there until they did. He sat there every day for over a month. That was in 1891, and when the Democratic National Convention opened in Chicago, in June of that year, the paper had to have some extra reporters so they gave him a job. Then an incredible thing happened. This cub reporter, who had never written a line for a newspaper in his life, was having a drink with the other reporters at the bar of the Auditorium Hotel; the other reporters were bemoaning the fact that no one knew who was going to be nominated. Dreiser had had a couple of cocktails and he wanted to show off, so he said, "I know who is going to be nominated. A dark horse, Senator McEnty of South Carolina." Just at that instant, Senator McEnty swung into the room and said, "Who does me the honor of mentioning my name?"

Dreiser confessed; and the Senator said: "That's fine. Let's have a drink." Then five minutes later, he invited Dreiser to have lunch and some more gin rickeys; and under their mellow influence, the Senator said: "I want you to go to Washington with me as my private secretary."

After lunch, McEnty said: "Listen boy—I'm going to let you in on a dark secret. Grover Cleveland is going to be nominated for President; and you are the first newspaper man to know it."

Dreiser was flabbergasted. He had only been a reporter for two days, and had gotten the biggest scoop of the year.

A few months after that, the *St. Louis Globe-Democrat* wired him to join its staff. Three months after that the *Globe-Democrat* dramatic editor resigned and Dreiser was given his work. He says he hasn't the faintest idea why they did it because he didn't know anything about the theatre.

One Monday night four shows opened in St. Louis, and Dreiser couldn't attend all of them—so he went to see one show and wrote reviews of the other three without seeing them. He wrote the reviews just as if he had been sitting in the front seat during the performance. He even made sneering remarks about the acting; and the next morning after these appeared in print, he learned that there had been a railway washout and the shows had never been in St. Louis at all.

He was so disgusted that he resigned from the paper.

I asked him to tell me the secret of his success and he said: "Just the mercy of God—that's all."

SNAKES IN THE ATTIC, MONKEYS ON THE CHANDELIERS—THAT'S HOME SWEET HOME TO DITMARS

WHEN the Bushmaster arrived in New York, thousands of people rushed up to the Bronx to see him. He was only a baby, six feet long, but in his sharp fangs he packed a load of swift and terrible death.

Raymond Ditmars, the man in charge of the New York Zoo, had been searching for a Bushmaster for twenty-five years; and when he finally got one, he had to force the "crittur" to eat. I inquired how—but he told me it's simple; all you have to do is pry open the viper's mouth and poke the meat down its throat with a stick!

And that's just the way Raymond Ditmars feels about snakes. He has handled thousands of them, but has never been bitten. Nevertheless, for people who don't get along so well with his scaly friends, he has cooperated in developing a serum—a serum that took many years to develop, and that has saved many thousands of lives.

When Ditmars was a boy, his father sent him to a military academy to prepare for West Point and a career in the army; but it was no use, for the call of wild things was already in his blood. Fired with boyish enthusiasm, he started out to make the biggest collection of snakes in New York—and he succeeded. He spent his week-ends hunting rattlers and copperheads along the Hudson

RAYMOND DITMARS
He fed his serpents from the cellars of Chinatown

River. He bought snakes, he traded for them, and he begged for them. The captain of a fruit boat gave him a boa constrictor, and he wrote to scientists in the West Indies; and traded American snakes for the reptiles that infest the jungles.

Finally his collection became so large and so dangerous that his mother gave him the entire upper floor of the house. Newspapers heard about it and wrote thrilling stories. Snake charmers and circus people came to see him; and his house became the sensation of the block.

In order to make money to buy food for his reptiles, he began studying stenography. His father read Dickens' novels aloud; and he practised by taking them down in shorthand. He now has a set of Dickens in shorthand which he treasures highly.

Later, when he became a newspaper reporter, he used to set traps in the basement of restaurants down in China-town and catch mice and rats to feed his vipers.

When New York City decided to build a large Zoo, Raymond Ditmars was hired immediately to take charge of the reptiles, and his mother fervently thanked God when her son moved all his rattlers and copperheads out of the house and took them to the new Zoo.

That was in 1899. Since then, New York has assembled one of the world's finest collections of animals; and Ray-mond Ditmars is now regarded as the world's greatest authority on snakes.

How much fun is a barrel of monkeys? Well, a few years ago Doctor Ditmars decided to keep a few monkeys in his home in Scarsdale; and one day while the family was away, these monkeys broke out of the cage and held high carnival. Climbing on top of the buffet, they made flying leaps and caught the chandelier that hung over the dining-room table. Nice doin'! It was just like swinging on a grapevine in the jungle. So they leaped and swung and did aerial stunts all over the place until they almost jerked the chandelier off the ceiling. They short-circuited the electric wires; and Doctor Ditmars says it's a wonder the house didn't catch fire and burn up. They climbed up on the piano and pounded the keys with a pair of old shoes. They smashed the chinaware, scattered pickles over the carpet, smeared cold cream on the mirrors, got into the drawers of the sewing-machine and took the thread off the spools and wound it all over the house. They turned the bureau drawers upside down and carried the frying pans out of the kitchen and put them under the beds upstairs. When the family returned, the place looked as if it had been struck by a hurricane.

And that, says Doctor Ditmars, is "how much fun a barrel of monkeys is."

A FIRE, AN ASTROLOGER, AND SOME
HORN-RIMMED GLASSES MADE
HIM THE RICHEST ACTOR
IN THE WORLD

MY FIRST sight of Harold Lloyd was a distinct shock. I should never have known him off the screen, but he says, for that matter, no one does. For example, on one occasion, he was at a party with a friend who wears glasses. (Lloyd himself never wears them off the screen.) This friend didn't resemble him at all; but everybody thought that the chap in the horn-rimmed glasses must be Harold Lloyd. The friend kept saying: "But I'm *not* Harold Lloyd. There he is." But the other guests thought he was joking.

I always thought of Harold Lloyd as being quiet and studious. But he isn't. I talked to him for hours and he kept laughing and bubbling over with enthusiasm. Spoiled? Not a bit of it. He is sincere and democratic.

He has nothing but contempt for superstitions—he thinks they smack of ignorance and the dark ages; but he admits that he has a few himself. For example, he won't go through a certain tunnel in Los Angeles because he believes it brings him bad luck. He always tries to go out of a building through the same door that he entered it, and he often carries a roll of "lucky" money.

HAROLD LLOYD
They told him he would never be a comedian

His latest hobby is painting landscapes; and he loves to mystify his friends with legerdemain and magic and card tricks. And he breeds dogs. He once had over seventy Great Danes barking and leaping all over the place.

He told me about a trifling thing that occurred when he was twelve years old—well, it seemed trifling at the time—but it changed the whole course of his life.

One day as he was drifting home from school in Omaha, Nebraska, he came across an astrologer standing on a street corner surrounded by colored charts. This astrologer claimed he could read your fortune by the stars. Little Harold listened, pop-eyed with excitement. Suddenly a fire engine dashed by, and the other boys ran after it. But he didn't. He kept listening to the astrologer. That was a strange thing for a boy to do and one of the men in the crowd noticed it. The fellow that noticed it was John Lane Connor, the leading man in the Burwood Stock Company of Omaha. He walked over to Lloyd, got acquainted with him and asked him if he knew of some nice place where an actor could get board and room. . . . Did he? . . . Harold leaped at the chance! He couldn't have been more thrilled if John L. Sullivan and Buffalo Bill had both wanted to board at his home. For years, he had been yearning and dreaming about being an actor himself some day.

He had even built a stage in the basement of his own home and written childish plays and acted in them and charged the neighboring kids three cents admission to see them. And now he was to have a real actor sitting across the table from him three times a day.

From this time on, whenever the local stock company in Omaha wanted someone to play a boy's part, Connor spoke up and got the job for Harold Lloyd.

Harold has never forgotten that kindness; he now has Connor in Hollywood taking entire charge of his fan mail.

Harold's mother was a dressmaker, and his father sold sewing machines. One day his father got smashed up in an automobile accident and hurt his back, and the insurance company paid him $3,500. That was a fortune, so he decided to pack up and leave the middle west and try his luck somewhere else. But where? The family was hopelessly divided between California and New York.

Finally Harold's father said: "Let's flip a coin. If it's heads, we'll go to California. If it's tails, we'll go to New York."

But heads came up, so the family moved to San Diego, and Harold did odd jobs about the theatre there and finally got a chance to play an extra bit in pictures. The first time he ever appeared before the camera, he was made up as an Indian and all he had to do was to hand a tray of food to some white people. He didn't think then that the movies would ever amount to anything. No one did. But finally he got so short of cash that he had to live in a tent, and he had only one nickel between himself and hunger; and he spent his last five cents for six greasy doughnuts sprinkled with powdered sugar. He decided to get a regular job in pictures if he could.

Day after day, he called at the casting offices; and day after day, he was turned away. He was desperate. He must get by that doorman. He noticed that at noon all the actors came out of the Universal lot and went across the road to a lunch counter, and he also noticed that the doorman didn't pay any attention to them when they came back with their grease paint on. So the next day, Harold Lloyd hid behind a billboard at noon, put on some make-up himself and slipped by the doorman in the crowd.

For days he mixed with the other actors inside the lot without having a job. They liked him and even pulled him through the dressing room windows so that he wouldn't have to bother with the doorman.

There was an actor by the name of Hal Roach who was playing small bits on this lot. He told Lloyd one day that his aunt had died and left him a little money so he was going to make pictures himself, comedies, and wanted Harold to join him.

So Harold started making one-reel comedies, started by wearing funny trousers and imitating Charlie Chaplin.

One day he picked up an idea that was worth a fortune to him—picked it up quite by accident. He was tired, so he drifted into a theatre and saw an actor with a straw hat and a pair of horn-rimmed glasses playing the part of a preacher. This actor wasn't trying to be funny; but he was really a scream. Lloyd decided then and there to make horn-rimmed glasses his trademark and to play the part that has since made him famous.

The funniest thing I know about Harold Lloyd is that he himself didn't know he was funny until he was twenty years old. Before that, he used to go around reciting Shakespeare. And when he first started making pictures, the directors told him he wasn't a comedian and never could be a comedian and they advised him to get out of pictures and make his living at something else. But he kept right on—and now he is the richest actor in all the world. In fact, he is the richest actor who ever lived.

DORIS DUKE

If she goes to buy a hat, two or three detectives watch
with pistols

HER PAPPY MADE $101,000,000.—BUT DIDN'T GET A "DINGED BIT OF FUN" OUT OF MONEY

THE richest girl in the world is married now—and worth $53,000,000. She has often been called the Poor Little Rich Girl because wherever she goes, reporters and cameramen pester the life out of her. She can't even go out and shop for a hat without two or three detectives, armed with pistols, trailing at her heels to protect her.

She has five enormous estates—four in America and one on the French Riviera. Her five thousand acre farm in Somerville, New Jersey, with its broad lawns and sparkling lakes and acres of rhododendrons and green houses, is one of the show places of the East.

Yet only a week before her marriage, she appeared at Palm Beach in a red wool bathing suit which she admitted was three years old. And in spite of her vast fortune, she could find no more beautiful setting for her wedding ceremony than a great fireplace with blazing logs.

How was the huge fortune amassed that makes Doris Duke the richest heiress in the world? Well, it was all made out of smoke—tobacco smoke.

The story of the Duke millions reaches back to the close of the Civil War. Those were bitter days for the South—armies had ravaged the land and the fields were barren and deserted. Suffering was intense. People boiled chestnuts and cotton seed to make a substitute for coffee and brewed a concoction of blackberry leaves and sassafras roots to take the place of tea. Even the earthen floor of smoke houses, saturated with the drippings of bacon, were dug up and boiled to get salt. Washington Duke, the grandfather of the richest girl in the world, had fought under Lee at Richmond and had suffered in the notorious Libby Prison. After Lee's surrender, he returned to his farm in Durham, North Carolina.

The Confederate government had given him a span of blind mules, decrepit with age and he had traded a $5. Confederate note to a Northern soldier for a half-dollar.

That was all Washington Duke had with which to face the future—fifty cents in silver, a pair of blind mules, some chain harness and two motherless boys.

Both the Confederate and the Northern armies had swept over the neighborhood and the hungry soldiers had stripped the fields bare of everything that could be eaten. The only thing they had left standing was some green tobacco. So he and his two boys, "Buck" and "Ben," harvested the tobacco, dried it, beat it with hickory sticks, packed it into bags, loaded it into a covered wagon, hitched up the pair of old, blind mules and started out to conquer the world—and the funny part of it is that they did conquer the world of tobacco, and built a tobacco empire that encircled the globe.

With their mules and covered wagon, they headed for the Southern part of the state where tobacco was scarce. They bartered tobacco for bacon and cotton. At night, they camped by the side of a road, fried bacon and sweet potatoes, and slept under the stars. This was a lot more fun than *raising* tobacco, so they decided to devote their lives to the business of *selling* tobacco.

But as time went on, they encountered fierce and savage competition. Hundreds of firms were making pipe tobacco—big, rich, powerful firms. James Buchanan Duke, the father of Doris Duke, knew that he had to do something different and do it at once—or he would be sunk. So he hit upon an idea that made him a hundred million dollars. He decided to make cigarettes. That may not sound so original today when Americans smoke one hundred and twenty-five billion cigarettes every year; but in 1881, it was revolutionary. Russians and Turks had been smoking cigarettes for generations, and British soldiers had brought them back from the Crimean War; but America, the land that gave tobacco to the world, had no cigarettes until 1867.

When "Buck" Duke started, cigarettes were rolled by hand. He perfected a machine that increased the manufacture from twenty-five hundred a day to one million a day. He designed the first practical cigarette package. All of you who can remember such brands as Meccas, Ziras, Sweet Caporals, or Turkish Trophies, will recall the cardboard box with the sliding case that "Buck" Duke designed.

He did a land-office business; and when Congress reduced the tax on tobacco, he stunned his competitors by slashing the price in half and flooding the market with cigarettes at five cents a box.

Then he began to look about for new worlds to conquer. He was only twenty-seven when he came to New York to establish another factory. He said to himself over and over, "If John D. Rockefeller can do what he is doing in oil, why can't I do it in tobacco?" So he plowed all his profits back into the business. Even while he was making $50,000. a year, he lived in a cheap little room in the Bowery and ate in the cheapest lunch carts.

Yet this man, who felt he couldn't afford to eat a fifty cent dinner, was sending his agents to every far-flung corner of the earth.

He himself slaved in his factory from early morning until late at night, supervising every step of the work from the raw leaf to the finished package.

He died worth $101,000,000. and he used to boast that he had made more millionaires than any other man in America. Yet he went to school for only four or five years. He once said: "A college education is all right for preachers and lawyers, but what use would it be to me? Superior brains are not necessary in business."

This is the way he explained his success. I am quoting his exact words now—"I have succeeded in business, not because I have more natural ability than many people who have not succeeded, but because I have applied myself harder and stuck to it longer. I know plenty of people who have failed to succeed in anything who have more brains than I have; but they lacked application and determination."

Curiously enough, this man felt that he himself didn't need an education, gave $40,000,000. to found a great University which bears his name today. It is Duke University in Durham, North Carolina, and one of its trustees is Doris Duke—probably the youngest University trustee in the world.

"Buck" Duke hated publicity, and he gave only one interview in his life. At that interview, the reporter asked him, "Mr. Duke, is there any satisfaction in just having a million dollars?"

"Buck" Duke shook his head and said, "Naw, not a dinged bit."

THE "PERFECT LOVER" WHO CHEWED TOBACCO, BIT HIS FINGER-NAILS, AND DRANK WINE OUT OF HUMAN SKULLS

WHAT was the perfect lover like a hundred years ago? What sort of man made our grandmothers' hearts go pit-a-pat and made our grandfathers, sitting by the fireside, twitch with a jealous apprehension? Who was the Don Juan, the Valentino, the Clark Gable of that far-off day?

The answer is easy. A hundred years ago there was no man in the world who could compete, so far as the ladies were concerned, with the romantic George Gordon, Lord Byron.

He was the greatest poet of his day. His influence changed the whole trend of literature in the nineteenth century. He wrote some of the gustiest romantic verse to be found in our anthologies, and some of the tenderest. He loved dozens of women, but strangest of all, he loved his own half-sister, and the scandal of their love shocked Europe and ruined her life. After they were driven apart, he wrote to her one of his loveliest poems:

> *If I should meet thee*
> *After long years,*
> *How should I greet thee?—*
> *With silence and tears.*

But the more notorious Byron became, the more the women worshipped him. They worshipped him so madly that when his wife finally left him because she couldn't stand his brutality any longer, half the women of Europe denounced her. These same women deluged Byron with poems and love-letters and locks of their hair. One famous English noble-woman, an aristocrat, brilliant and wealthy, a beauty with all of London at her dainty feet, dressed herself as a boy and stood in the street for hours in the pelting rain waiting for Byron, the perfect lover, to emerge from his sacred domicile. One woman lost her head over him so completely that she followed him all the way from England to Italy and pestered him until he finally gave up.

What was he like, this great paragon of lovers, this Valentino of a century ago? He had a deformed foot. He limped badly. He chewed his finger-nails. He chewed tobacco. He swashbuckled about in the broad daylight of 19th century Britain bristling with loaded pistols like a Chicago gangster. His temper was vicious. If people stared at him, his blood pressure rose twenty points, for he imagined they were staring at his deformed foot. This poet who was hailed as the perfect Romeo, loved to torture women. Two hours after the marriage ceremony, he informed his bride that he hated her, that he had married her only out of spite and that she would live to rue the day she first saw him. She did.

Their connubial bonds held for one year. To be sure, he never beat her but he smashed the furniture and brought his sweethearts into the house. His wife finally called in doctors to see if he was insane.

The country people who lived near his great Abbey told strange yarns: They said that all his servants were young girls—beautiful girls, girls with amiable dispositions. The country folks told how he and his guests dressed up as monks in long black cassocks and indulged in orgies that would have made Belshazzar's dinner parties sound like a W.C.T.U. breakfast. Amiable servant girls served the wine, and Byron and his friends drank it out of *human skulls*—scraped and polished until they shone like a full moon in the desert.

Byron, slender and graceful, was often compared to the Apollo Belvedere. His skin was so white that adoring females declared that he looked "like a beautiful alabaster vase lighted up from within." But they didn't realize what agonies he went through to look like that. They didn't know that every day of his life, and every hour, was a constant, irritating, and exhausting battle against fat. In order to remain slender and lovable, he endured a diet so fantastic that it has never hit even Hollywood.

For example, he ate only one meal a day, and that one meal frequently consisted of nothing but a little potato or rice with vinegar sprinkled over it. Wanting a change, he munched a handful of dry crackers and drank a glassful of soda-water. Talk about "alabaster lighted up from within"! The miracle is that he didn't look like a Chinese skeleton in the famine district. To keep down the hated fat, he went in for fencing, boxing, horseback-riding and swimming. And this man, the greatest poet of his age, was far prouder of the fact that he had swum the Hellespont than he was of his immortal verses. When he played cricket he wore seven vests. But even seven vests didn't sweat the fat off, so three times a week he had himself pummeled and mauled in a Turkish bath.

This fantastic dieting ruined his digestion; and, as a result, his bedroom reeked of pills and potions and patent medicines. It looked more like an apothecary's shop than the seductive bower of the world's greatest lover.

He suffered so horribly from nightmares that he resorted to laudanum. But even laudanum couldn't stifle his bad dreams, so he kept two loaded pistols beside his bed. In the quiet of the night, he would wake up yelling and gnashing his teeth, and would stride up and down the room brandishing pistols and daggers.

What a story he could have written for *True Confessions* magazine. Even the *Voice of Experience* would have been stumped by the problems of his bride.

The old Abbey in which Lord Byron had his nightmares was haunted by the ghost of a long-vanished monk who had once lived there. Byron swore that this blackhooded spectre often stalked past him in the corridor with a devastating eye. He beheld this terrible apparition on the eve of his ill-fated marriage. Years later, in Italy, he swore he saw the apparition of the poet Shelley walk into a wood. Shelley himself was miles away at that moment. And Byron knew it. Curiously enough, in a short time Shelley really was dead—drowned in a storm on a lake—and Byron with his own hands built the funeral pyre and burned the body.

He had another superstition that haunted him. A gypsy fortune-teller once warned him that he would die in his thirty-seventh year. He died three months after he had passed his thirty-sixth birthday. Byron believed a sinister curse doomed all his family. The thirty-sixth birthday, he swore, was fatal to people of his blood. Some modern biographers are even inclined to agree with him for Byron's father died at the age of thirty-six, and Byron's daughter, whose life was almost exactly like her father's, also died on the eve of her thirty-six birthday.